Delius

THE GREAT COMPOSERS

DELIUS

by

ERIC FENBY

FABER AND FABER
3 Queen Square
London

First published in 1971
by Faber and Faber Limited
3 Queen Square London WC1
Printed in Great Britain by
Latimer Trend & Co Ltd Plymouth

ISBN 0 571 09296 9

Contents

Illustrations

Illustrations

LINE ILLUSTRATIONS

Music Examples

9

Acknowledgements

I am most grateful to the following for their kindness in allowing me to quote from copyright material: to Boosey and Hawkes Music Publishers Limited for the extract from Sonata No. 3 for Violin and Piano; to Novello and Company Limited for the opening theme of Elgar's Violin Concerto; to Oxford University Press for fragments from *Life's Dance* and an extract from Gerard Bunk's piano arrangement of *On Hearing the First Cuckoo in Spring*; to Schott and Company Limited for Percy Grainger's choral setting of *Brigg Fair*; to Universal Edition (London) Limited for extracts from *Paris*, *The Walk to the Paradise Garden* from the opera *A Village Romeo and Juliet*, *Appalachia*, *Sea-Drift* and *Brigg Fair*; and to Dr. Philip Emanuel, the legal trustee of the Delius Trust, for permission to make piano reductions of extracts from the unpublished manuscripts of *Hiawatha*, *Paa Vidderne*, *Scènes Parisiennes* and *The Dance Goes On*, and quote passages from three letters by Delius to Grieg, one from Sinding, and reproduce a page in facsimile of a letter to Granville Bantock.

I also owe my thanks to Mr. Hugh Alderman for telling me about Jacksonville, Florida, in the 1880's; to Dr. Lionel Carley, Archivist to the Delius Trust, for his photograph of Jelka Delius's bronze head of her husband; to The Radio Times Hulton Picture Library for the photograph of the Deliuses at the Langham Hotel in 1929; and to my old friend Philip Oyler, formerly of Grez-sur-Loing, for his beautiful photographs of the village in the 1930's, and to Mr. Ronald Moore, of the London Symphony Orchestra, for his photograph of Solano Grove.

I

Beginnings in Bradford

Music—especially orchestral music—in the industrial towns of northern England in the latter half of the nineteenth century owed much to cultivated music-lovers among the German immigrant population. In Bradford, for instance, in the eighteen-eighties it was Julius Delius, the composer's father, who contrived the first visit of the Hallé Orchestra to the newly-built St. George's Hall and helped in founding the Subscription Concerts which continue to this day. Julius, like many a Delius before him, had left the family seat at Bielefeld in the province of Westphalia to try his luck abroad, and joined his brother Ernst in the wool trade in Manchester. Eventually he had become a naturalized Englishman and set up on his own in Bradford, marrying Elise Krönig, also from Bielefeld, who was then seventeen and half his age. Their fourth child and second son, Fritz Theodor Albert Delius, was born on 29th January 1862.

The family were occupying temporary quarters at No. 6 Claremont across the road whilst the house next door to their real home at No. 1 was being annexed. Thus prophetically, it would seem, Fritz began life as the odd one out amidst the fourteen children of Julius and Elise—two of whom died in infancy—and grew up to be an odd man out and remained so to the end. His boyhood was carefree but constrained by a father whose every word was law in the comfortable, prosperous Delius household. He had violin lessons from the age of seven from a member of the Hallé Orchestra and played the piano as yet by ear, making up little descriptive pieces to amuse the family and their friends. There was no attempt, that he could recall, to write down these juvenile improvisations and nothing of the prodigy about him.

Claremont in those days backed on to the moors where Fritz used to wander far beyond home and usually with Max, a younger brother; so Julius bought the boys two ponies. 'I loved nothing better than a day in the saddle, alone if I could, on the moors to Ilkley. What stillness! It was there

I began to feel more and more intuitively that I was going to do something worthwhile with my life; what, I really didn't know!'

This feeling had led him blindly as a boy but gradually his eyes were opened to the truth implied in Goethe's remark that 'to *do* something one must first *be* something'. Neither his teachers nor his schooling had thrown any light, apparently, in guiding him to even a dawning of what those 'somethings' might possibly be. 'I disliked all subjects except geography and languages and made no impression whatever at school. I wasn't a very apt pupil either at the International College at Isleworth; my father had sent me there on a three-year course to prepare me for the family wool-business. All I could do was to come out top of the batting averages at cricket! Back in Bradford I hated the place; its straight-laced proprieties and provincial smugness! Everything seemed at variance with what in my flounderings I wanted from life!'

For almost five years on leaving college Fritz was an unwilling apprentice to the wool trade in Bradford and then in Chemnitz, Saxony. He made fitful attempts to apply himself, but his trips abroad as his father's agent relapsed into pleasurable excursions—especially to Scandinavia—and his dismissal was inevitable. The climax came when he had begged his father to allow him to take up music. Julius was adamant and would not hear of it.

Tensions driving them to this clash had been mounting through Fritz's later teens. It is remarkable, too, that they should have emerged from so musical an environment. Wilfulness, a male trait—so I am told—of the Deliuses, aggravated their relationship.

Julius was clearly informed in judgment on matters connected with the musical profession. He had always insisted on expert tuition as each of his children was ready to learn whichever instrument they cared to choose. This was surely from other motives than to indulge his passionate hobby of chamber music though it was Hobson's choice for the older ones. His sole objection to Fritz's decision—or so the composer continued to allege—was that music as a profession was demeaning to a gentleman, a view by no means then uncommon in middle-class society in England. Fritz's eldest brother, Ernest, had already been packed off to a New Zealand sheep farm to prevent his becoming an orchestral cellist! Admittedly he was an unstable fellow and Fritz's record was little better.

Fritz's abilities were known to Julius who led the family string quartet in which Fritz played second violin in works by Haydn, Mozart and Beethoven. Famous artists visiting Bradford were usually engaged to play in the drawing-room, and at one of these *conversaziones* Fritz had been called upon to deputise with Joachim the violinist and Piatti the cellist. If, as is said, he earned their praise, it can have counted for nothing in Julius's ruling. Nor does Hans Sitt, Fritz's teacher in Chemnitz, appear to have influenced him either; the question of a career in composition as yet had not arisen.

The painful quarrel went on for weeks and the two were barely on speaking terms. Fritz's favourite sister, Clare, took his part courageously and Mr. Sucksmith, the warehouse foreman, often hid him among the wool bales. 'Clare saved me more than once at lunch on Sundays after church when my father questioned me about the sermon. I used to vault the churchyard wall as the family filed into the porch. There was a big stone on which I would sit facing the moor and then I'd slip back into the procession after the service.'

Clare had shared his holidays with their grandmother at Bielefeld and his pranks on the Yorkshire coast at Filey. Eventually a whole railway coach was needed to transport the Delius household to the seaside!

Fritz's position was obscure and unenviable. Disturbed by those inner promptings that before long were to lead him on to compose, he had no understanding of how to improve his lack of general musicianship, now so obvious to himself, and nobody to whom to turn for advice. But leave Bradford he must. His urgent problem without delay was to find some form of easy livelihood affording daily leisure for study. Fritz arrived at the attractive solution of orange growing in Florida. What a colourless story his would have been as a student in our present age!

He explained to his father that his friend, Charles Douglas, would accompany him and share in the project; the two had been school-chums at the Old Bradford Grammar School and the Douglases were neighbours of the Deliuses and well known throughout the West Riding of Yorkshire.

Julius submitted with good grace at last and instructed his lawyer to secure a lease on a suitable holding in Florida. Meanwhile with an enthusiasm which disconcerted Fritz, Julius fitted him out with expensive tropical kit.

II

Adventure in America

In March of 1884 Charles and Fritz sailed from Liverpool in the Cunard liner *Gallia*. Their immediate destination was New York, but unlike most British emigrants of the time they were bound ultimately for a remote spot outside the sphere of British rule—Solano Grove, formerly an old Spanish orange plantation on the east bank of the St. Johns River about forty miles south of Jacksonville which stands some fifteen miles inland from the north-east coast of the Florida peninsula. An improbable place one would surely have thought in which to take the initial step of devoting oneself to a life of music, for this by now was the secret aim of the more singular character of the two.

They continued their journey south from New York in a steamer of the Mallory line for at least another thousand miles to the port of Fernandina, a haunt of pirates and smugglers in the days when Florida was a Spanish colony before joining the United States in 1821. On landing they went by train to Jacksonville, then a thriving winter resort of about ten thousand inhabitants. Twenty years earlier it had been almost obliterated during the Civil War. Its wharves and docks now hummed with the trade of its rapidly growing industries; its theatre, new hotels and boarding-houses told of its attraction to affluent pleasurers. Jasmine, wisteria and purple hyacinths smothered its buildings in a patchwork of colours spilling over into the great river in the sunlight.

Here they took legal possession of the property and travelled by river paddle-boat for the thirty odd miles to Picolata, the nearest landing-stage. They still had a few more miles to go on a rutted cart track through the forest which brought them to a clearing. So this was the thriving orange-farm—a desolate, verandahed shack and a wilderness of overgrown orange trees!

Laughter saved the situation. The shack at least could be made comfortable; it was solidly built of cypress wood; there were four rooms with brick fireplaces and a small kitchen at the rear; the verandah faced a huge magnolia and a gigantic oak by the water's edge.

Fritz had never imagined a river as wide as this so far from the sea, nor such a variety of shrubs in the teeming undergrowth. Grey veils of Spanish moss hung like delicate films of gauze enclosing every tree. He was fascinated. The play of light through the dense woods touched the scene with a mystery he was later to evoke in music inspired by the memory of these surroundings.

For a time things went well, though Charles was often disturbed by his friend's remote self-centredness. They did their own cooking and learned from their Negro overseer the ways of orange-growing. Fritz practised his violin regularly but this did not suffice. He was impatient to come to grips with the craft of music itself and capture the sounds that sang in his mind. He could write down with accuracy their melodic shape but could not define a harmonic background without the aid of a piano. This only increased his restlessness. He began to neglect his share of the chores and this led to tiffs with Charles. Their future together now seemed uncertain. The break came sooner than either can have expected.

Charles fell ill; they suspected malaria, so Fritz set off to Picolata to catch the steamer to Jacksonville intending to return in the evening with medicine. A doctor not being immediately available, Charles and his plight it seems were forgotten in Fritz's anxiety to buy or hire a piano!

Fritz had been directed to West Bay Street and was trying pianos in the music store in his personal and instinctive way of playing endless strings of chords. A passer-by struck by this strange procedure went in to satisfy his curiosity. He was Thomas Ward, organist of the church of the Immaculate Conception, who had left his post in Brooklyn, New York, in search of better health. The two were quickly on friendly terms; Ward invited Fritz to a meal and they continued their talk past midnight. Here for the first time in his life Fritz had met a kindred spirit discussing the technical knowledge he sought. Nothing could have been more opportune. Fritz confided his musical difficulties; Ward outlined a course to meet them urging him to begin at once. Three days were spent in Jacksonville absorbed by this chance acquaintance.

Help had been brought from Picolata and Charles had almost recovered by Fritz's return. The two now agreed to part; Charles moved out to a neighbouring grove and Ward joined Fritz in the tiny shack fulfilling his duties as organist in Jacksonville on Sundays.

Ward, at heart a man of tradition, was puzzled at first by his erratic pupil, yet he gradually came to divine in him something of infinitely greater capacity

The cover and first page of Delius's *Zum Carnival*, published in 1892

ZUM CARNIVAL.

Fritz Delius

than the response revealed in his written exercises. There is nothing in the quality of their execution to suggest that a remarkable talent would eventually emerge. But Ward understood him thoroughly. He allowed him to sample and experience rather than master traditional techniques, with the end purpose always in mind of guiding him to think for himself in sounds.

For six, breathless, humid months he instilled the habit of orderly work, making him learn entirely by 'doing', then correcting and revising. Finally he went back to Jacksonville heartened and feeling physically stronger: this, unhappily, was not to last.

The next three months Fritz lived alone except for a devoted Negro servant who insisted on sleeping outside his door rather than in his bunk in the loft. This, he told me many years later, was the most decisive period of his life. 'Orange growing as a means of livelihood had no more interest whatever for me. All that mattered was the silence of the grove for hour after hour of uninterrupted work. From then on I wanted to be a composer.'

The unusual occurrence of a piano being unloaded from the steamer at Picolata brought Fritz to the notice of Jutta Mordt, a professional singer and the Norwegian wife of an Englishman, a Lieutenant Bell, who had lived for some time in the vicinity. She introduced him to the music of Grieg and advised him on his operatic projects long after he had left Florida. Grieg's music provided an impetus now that Ward was gone. Several songs and little piano pieces were written at this period. One of them, a polka, *Zum Carnival*, was dedicated to William Jahn, Junior, a friend and the son of a Jacksonville music teacher who secured its publication locally and gave Fritz his first formal instruction on the piano.

The carnival spirit was much in the air at Jacksonville in the winter months. Electricity, the latest novelty, had transformed the evening social scene. Fritz was in demand as a solo violinist. A press report of one of these concerts at which he had played Raff's *Cavatina* described him as 'a likeable, attractive young man with charming manners, neat and well-dressed'. The pull of city against rural life as yet did not disturb him.

Alligators in the creeks and swamps had been a pest that year round Picolata. Fritz went on shooting parties with the Negroes, hunting them at night by lantern. Exciting as these adventures may have been, his lasting impressions of the wild life about him gave rise to a growing firm conviction of the supremacy of instinct and the wonder of it all, a conviction that was to change his outlook both on music and on life.

The protective instincts of mating creatures fascinated him particularly. 'I had borrowed a horse and gone out shooting and foolishly dismounted to

Above left, Fritz (later Frederick) Delius, *c.* 1865; *above right*, Julius Delius, the composer's father

Below, Claremont, Bradford, Delius's birthplace

Delius, *c.* 1874

Delius and his mother in 1884

smoke a cigar. The heat was sweltering! I let the horse loose; suddenly it disturbed two snakes in the undergrowth; it reared and bolted off down the track! I shot one snake and chased the horse with the other snake at my heels. I turned, cocked my gun and fired: it was empty! Luckily I got a foot in the stirrup, mounted and galloped back home with the snake still after me! I dashed indoors, seized a gun and shot it as it poised itself at the foot of the verandah.' He was silent for a while and then added, 'I couldn't sleep that night thinking of the instinctive bond of that snake with its mate!' Trivial as this recollection might seem it was plain that it had meant much to him.

Fritz was drawn to the black people when they sang improvised harmonies to their folk-songs after dusk in neighbouring orange groves. If in old age he was over-inclined to romanticise these reminiscences, they had certainly influenced his music when he came to write *Florida*, his first orchestral work, his Negro opera *Koanga* and his *Appalachia* variations. Though grounded in European musical art-forms these works are saturated with a quality of sound not heard before in the orchestra, or rarely since, a quality derived from and redolent of Negro hymnology and folk-song.

In Bradford Fritz's silence could no longer be defended. Six months had passed without a word. Julius demanded an explanation; none was forthcoming. News of the breach between Charles and Fritz had already reached the Douglas home and was causing estrangement between the two families. A Mr. Sucksmith was directed to sail to Florida to report on Fritz's activities. For reasons best known to himself, he faltered embarrassed at the last moment and a Mr. Tattersfield was sent instead briefed by Julius to persuade Fritz to set up as an agent for the firm in Florida. Tattersfield was to complete the provisional contract and buy Solano Grove outright.

Fritz refused to have anything to do with the first of these proposals. Ward was alarmed by his predicament. Fritz, he argued, should go to Leipzig to study at the Konservatorium. Delius needed finer tuition, Ward felt, than he himself could give. Events were to prove otherwise. The next move could not have been more unexpected. 'I was sitting one day on the verandah after a meal when a boat pulled in by the river bank and a bearded, scruffy-looking fellow hailed me—"Hello Fritz! Hello! Don't you know me? I'm Ernest—your brother Ernest!" I was speechless for a moment! "Ernest!" I shouted back, "Ernest! I thought you were in New Zealand!" Ernest explained that he had tired of sheep-farming and had hitch-hiked to Florida to look me up!'

This indeed was a gift from the Gods! With Ernest already on the spot, he might be willing to take over the property. Fritz was not long in planning his move. He would work his passage to Bradford in stages and make a final appeal to his father. Ernest needed no persuading; he was always willing to try something new.

So in midsummer of 1885 Fritz left Solano Grove and a broken-hearted Negro servant. 'Poor fellow! He implored me to take him with me. I've never known such devotion. I really believe he'd be with me now!'

Fritz moved into Jacksonville hoping to find pupils with the help of Ward. 'I hadn't much luck as a music teacher there but, fortunately, they wanted a tenor at the Synagogue. For some reason I was appointed. Ward must have cracked me up as an organist for I was sometimes asked to play the services. I was quite hopeless on the organ; especially on the pedal-board! Then after a few weeks at the Synagogue I applied for a post in Danville, Virginia, to teach the daughters of a Professor Ruckert in return for my keep and such other pupils as he could get. The Chief Rabbi, the dearest old fellow, gave me a glowing testimonial and I was accepted. Ward was very upset when I left. We corresponded, but I never saw him again.'

Fritz enjoyed himself in Danville. The people were friendly and his employer ideal. More important still by far, he was five hundred miles nearer Bradford. A friend of the Ruckerts, Professor Phifer, found him additional teaching at the Roanoke Female College and even pleaded his cause with Julius. Several of his pupils on the violin were the daughters of wealthy tobacco planters; one at least had set her heart on Fritz. 'Her father took me aside one day and offered me a full partnership in his business if I would stay and marry her!'

Danville could not contain him long. He had arrived there in the middle of the night with only a dollar left in his pocket after a journey by sea to Charleston and then by train through South Carolina. His performance of the Mendelssohn Violin Concerto had secured his local reputation and brought him more pupils than he could take. But as soon as he had saved his fare to New York and enough to keep him for a few days he announced regretfully that he must leave.

His movements now seem impossible to trace. I did not question him about this episode nor about any detail of his life. Such things as I know about him he told me entirely of his own accord, as did his wife. Perhaps after all it was better that way; otherwise had I been tiresomely inquisitive, I fear I should not have remained in his household for the six years before he died.

The news of Fritz's financial gains as a violin teacher in Danville in the letters of the admirable Phifer had meanwhile so impressed his father that he relented, but on one condition. Fritz must return to America after a year at Leipzig to exploit his teaching success still further. A lead to his whereabouts was made through Phifer, and Fritz was contacted and enabled to sail in June of 1886 for Liverpool and Bradford. Doubt has been cast upon the assertion that he had supported himself for a while as a church organist in New York. Yet I remember his saying on one occasion that despite his ineptitude on the instrument, it had saved him in Jacksonville and New York.

III

Leipzig and Two Friendships

That Fritz was a failure at Leipzig Konservatorium was neither his fault nor that of the authorities. His position was quite impracticable. Supposedly intent on a career as a teacher of the most difficult instrument of all—the violin, his heart was set on composition which demands no less a servitude but a different type of apprenticeship. Hans Sitt, his former teacher at Chemnitz and now on the staff of the Konservatorium, resumed as his tutor on the violin, and Professors Reinecke and Jadassohn extended the range of his studies with Ward in strict counterpoint to fugue. Their classes in musical analysis, however, served only to increase his antipathy to the music of those classical masters from whom he had begun to recoil in Bradford.

It is significant that Fritz made no lasting friendships with his student contemporaries at the Konservatorium; it is remarkable, too, that with so little to show in support of his abilities Grieg was so obviously impressed by his qualities and admitted him into an immediate companionship along with his countryman Christian Sinding. But they could surely never have dreamt that here in process of finding himself was one of music's supreme originals.

At the time of their meeting Grieg was already at the height of his powers and had long been lionized at Leipzig for his superb playing of his concerto with the old Gewandhaus Orchestra; he was conductor of the Philharmonic concerts in Christiania and now in his middle forties. Sinding, who had left the Konservatorium, had won renown as a talented performer of his own fluent piano music; he was just thirty. Fritz, the unknown first-year student, was barely in his middle twenties! Clearly musical life for Fritz began outside the Konservatorium.

With Nikisch and Mahler conducting at the opera house Wagner had become his musical god. There were sleepless nights upon performances of *Tristan*, and arguments and discussions after Brahms and Tchaikovsky had directed their orchestral works in the fine new Konzerthaus.

Imagine the impact of these powerful minds so compelling in individual mastery. Yet Fritz was not to be deflected; he followed his instinct, characteristically, pursuing the music that sang within him, working through his influences rather than avoiding them; he finished his first extended work, *Florida*, a suite for orchestra, and heard it realised in sound at a private performance for a barrel of beer! 'I learnt more in that half-hour than from all my months at the Konservatorium!' In fairness, for all that, it must be added that his attendances in class had been so perfunctory that he was refused a diploma on completing his course.

Grieg, with a persuasion unmatched in his music, had somehow prevailed upon Julius in London to support Fritz for one more year and even allow him to devote it to composing! This, it was agreed, was to be spent in Europe. His uncle Theodor in Paris offered to provide him with a *pied-à-terre* following his summer holiday in Norway mountain-climbing with Grieg and Sinding.

The three, for some years, were rarely out of touch. Fritz writes to Grieg from St. Malo in October, 1888: 'Hearty thanks for your dear letter which gave me such pleasure. I definitely believe that mankind has instinct. My instinct has seldom led me astray; my reason often. When I first met you it was not just mere instinct for I had already been acquainted so long with you through your music. A poet can disguise himself (I believe) but a composer must show himself or nothing at all.' He then tells Grieg of the songs he has written 'in the way which seemed most natural to me' and proposes to discuss them at their next meeting—. 'I attach so much to your criticism. . . . You must certainly see Paris. It is ten times more beautiful than London. . . . I would prefer to live rather alone, that is, in not too big a place; one enjoys life even more. Do you know what I'm intending to do?— please don't faint— to live in Norway eight months in the year and four in Leipzig or Paris. When I come to Norway I will look out for a nice place where I can live and work quietly. . . . Streets and smoke deform your ideas. One must breathe pure air before one can think purely. I feel well in body and spirit when nature is beautiful. When you come to Paris I will look after you and promise you a wonderful time. My uncle is a splendid fellow. In Paris I cannot do anything sensible, the surroundings mitigate against it.' Clearly he was beginning to model himself on the ways of painters and writers he met rather than of composers; he sought inspiration in the countryside as they were doing; he realized that the attractions of city life were impeding the development of his natural aptitude as a composer. But had he the will to resist them? Fritz did not find his own solution until the turn of the century.

And again to Grieg from St. Helier, Jersey: 'I saw a lot of Sinding . . . I also heard a rehearsal of his symphony. The first movement is the best in my opinion. The Scherzo is also very good. I like movements two and four less . . . the whole symphony doesn't hold together and is too thickly orchestrated. . . .'

A note from Sinding to Fritz is revealing: 'You are indeed a devil for work. In addition to all you've already done this year— another string quartet!'

Sinding was referring to a tone poem for orchestra *Hiawatha*; a recitation (to words by Ibsen) with orchestra *Paa Vidderne*; a *Pastorale* for violin and orchestra; and an unfinished work for orchestra *Rhapsodic Variations* all written in 1888.

On Sinding's intervention and the evidence of this industry both as composer and as a person of integrity, the authorities of Leipzig Konservatorium later awarded Fritz his diploma.

IV

The Odd Man Out

Fritz was to live eight years in Paris at the end of that period of vision and extravagance which must have been an enviable experience for any young artist of malleable temperament in the last decades of the nineteenth century. The joyous 'new eye' for the mystery of light had revealed its magic on natural things and seduced painting from its former conventions to sheer delight in the poetry of paint. Rapid brush-strokes of personal impression sought to capture on canvas for ever some elusive moment of visual felicity. Even today with eyes accustomed through actual contact or good reproductions, there is always a pleasurable jolt to the senses on suddenly coming upon these paintings, having approached them through galleries of earlier masterpieces. The transient 'glances' of Pissarro, Monet, Sisley and Renoir at country landscape, the contemporary pageantry round the Seine, the cafés, the boulevards and parks, and the truthful delineations of character in shop, ballet and bohemian life by Degas and Toulouse-Lautrec, these and others by their example confirmed in Fritz his instinct to withdraw and avoid for the most part the company of musicians. He wanted to do something similar in music but needed to find the technical means of projecting his imagination; the techniques he had acquired at Leipzig were useless for his purpose.

Fritz had tasted Parisian life the year before going off to Florida, and now that his practical affairs were assured through the further generosity of Uncle Theodor, he rented a chalet of two rooms at Ville d'Avray, a little village on the outskirts of Paris where Corot had loved to paint. He describes the little house to Grieg in an undated letter in the autumn of 1888: '. . . it stands quite alone on the bank of a small lake in a wood. So I am at work again. Next door there is a small restaurant where I eat. It is really wonderful here. Nobody comes and all around are woods and hills. One would think one is a hundred miles from Paris!' He visited Bradford the following April and later Norway to stay with the Griegs at Troldhaugen and Jendeboden and then moved to Croissy, still within easy reach of Paris. After eighteen months he finally settled for the next six years in a flat at 33 Rue Ducoüédic, Montrouge, Paris.

His friends of both sexes throughout these years—with a strong attraction to Scandinavians—were a truly amazing assortment of characters, including Strindberg, Gauguin and Munch. Already a man much given to extremes he engaged in adventurous alternations between the decorous society of his uncle's circle and the low life of Montmartre. He worked hard the while at two operas, *Irmelin* and *The Magic Fountain*, and completed the first act of a third, *Koanga*. He had written the libretti of these first two operas, doubtless in deference to Wagner's practice, but happily he abandoned this dual role.

Obsessed as he was by Scandinavian literature Fritz was even more deeply stirred by the works of the German philosopher, Nietzsche. They drew him to a young painter no less imbued. Her name was Jelka Rosen. She came from an old Schleswig-Holstein family remarkable for its distinguished diplomats; her father had been at the German Embassy in Belgrade when she was born. As a child she had travelled much with her parents throughout Europe and the Near East where she had picked up several languages quite naturally; she had been brought up more plainly than Fritz though as strictly; on her father's death she had persuaded her mother to move to Paris and allow her to paint.

She had seen Fritz often from the window of her *pension* as he passed by regularly on his way with Gauguin to a little café which catered for artists. Gauguin wore wooden sabots and made such a clattering on the cobblestones that she grew to anticipate his appearances. Fritz by comparison looked an aristocrat—tall, and always very smart. Eventually they met at a friend's studio. After a meal came the customary music; Jelka sang some songs by Grieg; Fritz was silent but polite and offered to show her some of his own. Two days later he went to her studio and accompanied himself in a light tenor voice whilst she stood beside him enthralled by their freshness, especially *Twilight Fancies*. 'I knew there could be no one else for me.'

Fritz had no such exclusive intentions and though he took her for country walks and played his most recent work to her, she was aware of his attentions to other women some of whom she disapproved. Yet she sensed a bond between them, his interest in her paintings and prospects of exhibiting. She spent her summers at Grez-sur-Loing, a little village beyond Fontainebleau, some forty kilometres south of Paris. Fritz had come down to Bourron nearby to discuss some changes in the libretto of *Koanga* that Keary, an author, was

The composer with his four younger sisters in 1888

Below, Solano Grove, St. John's, Florida, *c.* 1939

Delius with a friend, probably Charles Douglas, in 1884
Below, a game of cards with (*left to right*) Nina and Edvard Grieg, Johann Halvorssen, Frederick Delius and Christian Sinding in Leipzig, 1888

preparing for him and had walked over to see her at the Poule d'Eau, an inn much favoured then by artists. After some refreshments they had taken a boat and rowed up the river under the bridge and pulled into the bank of an overgrown garden. The owner, an eccentric, the Marquis de Carzeaux, had allowed Jelka to paint there; he was away at this time and the house shuttered. Fritz was enchanted by the place. He was quieter, she noticed, and more restless than usual. Suddenly he turned to her and said, 'Jelka, I could work here!'—and soon was strolling across the fields to catch the train back to Paris.

She saw him frequently in Paris that autumn. Then, near Christmas, he told her his plans to go to Florida for several months to consider the prospect of growing tobacco as the orange crops had been a failure. He was taking his vagabond fiddler-friend Jebe—a very disquieting thought for Jelka. But she was not one to be discouraged by this. She would solve this private emotional crisis in her own way through her painting.

That spring she heard that the Marquis had been swindled in a notorious case—the talk of Paris—and was anxious to sell the property at Grez; the purchase had to be made in cash. All her best work had been done in that garden. Paris now meant nothing to her. Gradually, she said, the idea grew uppermost—she must somehow buy the place herself! But she had only half the sum required from her father's small inheritance. Finally after incredible wrangling her mother agreed to lend her the balance on condition that Ida Gerhardi, her closest friend, and also a painter, shared the house with her.

V

Postcard from Paris

By the spring of 1897 Jelka and Ida were installed at Grez with Marie, a shrewd, gnarled Breton peasant as cook-housekeeper-gardener-protectress. The house was a warren of tiny rooms and they had little furniture between them, but Marie was resourceful and counted every sou. Their brief painting idyll of undisturbed work was shattered abruptly early that summer by the arrival of a postcard: Fritz, it read, was back in Paris and coming down next day for the weekend. That was the first she had heard of him for months!

Whatever was said or left unsaid in the female conference which ensued, Grez was thereafter to be his home and place of work for the rest of his life. Jelka herself went so far as to say that the sound of his composing at the piano whilst she and Ida were at their easels seemed a natural accompaniment to their household and even won over the redoubtable Marie.

Fritz's finances were very low. The trip to Florida had yielded little but talk of a possible business partnership. His father's remittance had ceased by agreement in exchange for the deeds of Solano Grove which had only just been assigned to him. He had had nothing for three years from his uncle Theodor through female intrigue in which he was blameless. This rift was even more unfortunate. Theodor had financed a rehearsal and performance of *Sur les Cimes*, an orchestral work first heard in Oslo, when repeated at the Monte Carlo concerts in 1893. Aunt Albertine, always ready with advice, had made Fritz a small gift annually when Theodor had stopped his allowance. There was a possible commission in the offing, but Jelka's main concern, however, was in trying to convert him to a more normal routine instead of working all hours of the night.

Already in his early formative period Fritz had established his own habit of work guided by the instinct of the moment. Thus he had several works on the stocks all in various stages of completion. Whenever he forced this natural approach he felt he was not being true to himself. He relied on an

30

ebbing and flowing of instinct. As soon as instinct began to wane in face of the next move ahead, rather than substitute intellect for instinct, he put the particular score aside and took up another work afresh till the same predicament urged him to cease. He never doubted the return of instinct to lead him on to the final bar. A piano concerto in three movements, the third act of *Koanga* and *Seven Danish Songs* for voice and orchestra occupied him in this manner until the end of the summer.

Still more significant than any of these inventions was his first draft of Zarathustra's *Night-Song* for baritone and piano. Jelka again: 'He had been working later than usual one night and called Ida and me up to his part of the house to hear something new he said he'd just written. When we heard Nietzsche's words as he sang the refrain and saw how they affected him as he played, we knew it was music of deep import, beyond anything he had done before.' It was plain as she spoke how much this music had meant to her then in determining her ultimate relationship with Delius.

Gunnar Heiberg, the Norwegian playwright, confirmed his commission for Fritz to write the music to his comedy *Folkeraadet*, a piece of political lampoonery. Fritz had completed the score by October and left Grez for Christiania to conduct the first performance. University students stampeded the play and uproar followed upon Fritz's ingenious parodying of their National Anthem. A blank shot was fired at him from a pistol and he dropped his baton and dashed from sight. He once recalled with a wry smile the clamour afterwards outside his hotel and how, as he peeped from behind a curtain, he saw the great figure of Ibsen emerge elbowing his way through the angry crowd. 'We're only barbarians in the north!' he growled when later he asked Delius to join him over his whisky. The play was a success eventually and Fritz was absolved from ill-intent.

The following month he returned through Germany breaking his journey at Elberfeld where, due to the zeal of Ida Gerhardi, he heard another performance of his *Over the Hills and Far Away*. It had been carefully prepared by Dr. Hans Haym who became his foremost champion forthwith until the ascendancy of Sir Thomas Beecham. Public reception was so adverse that Haym was cautioned by his committee to desist from similar outrages. Looking through the score of this orchestral piece one can scarcely imagine the state of mind that considered it so offensive. Fritz preserved exterior calm in face of these hostilities.

Back in Grez he took up the sketch of Zarathustra's *Night-Song* and arranged it for baritone solo, men's chorus and orchestra, one of the very few occasions on which he worked from a preliminary piano score. Otherwise

An extract from Delius's first orchestral work, *Florida*

Auprès de la Plantation
(Danse Nègre)

C

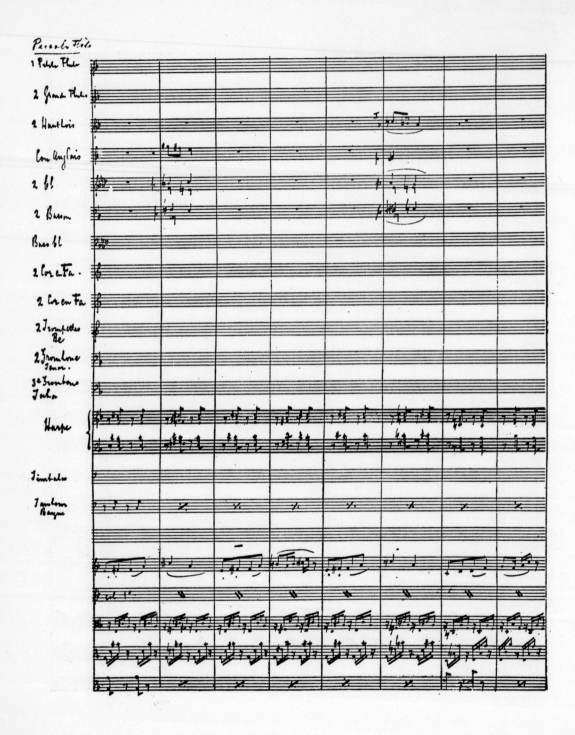

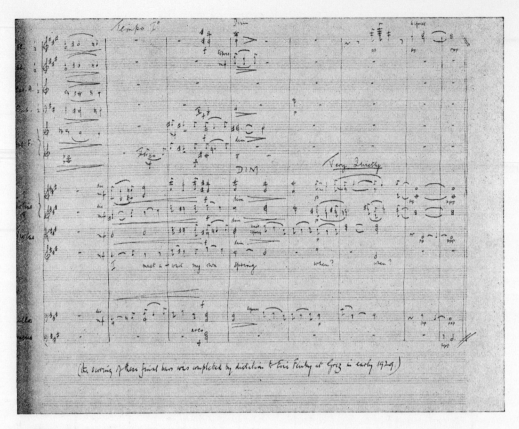

Revised ending of 'Let Springtime come, then' orchestrated by dictation to
Eric Fenby for the Delius Festival 1929

his music involving the orchestra was usually conceived straightway as such
and finished in instrumental detail as far as he had gone. His preoccupation
with orchestration is understandable at this stage for he had heard the effect
of his writing for orchestra but four times hitherto! Each time had been a
revelation—'especially of what not to do!'

He then attempted more fluent invention (which reveals his interest in
Strauss's scoring) in a tone-poem for orchestra *The Dance Goes On* (the first
version of *Life's Dance*) and wrote more songs to words by Nietzsche.

Again, at a most crucial time of his life, Providence sustained his resolution
to do nothing but go on composing music when every one but Jelka, Uncle
Theodor included, advised him to return to America at once and set up as a
teacher of the violin. Happily they were reconciled just before Theodor's
sudden death later in 1898, and Delius found himself richer by a legacy of
about one thousand pounds.

36

Postcard from Paris

The most tangible result of this windfall was the purchase of Gauguin's *Nevermore* for the sum of roughly twenty pounds. This was more than Gauguin's price so both were satisfied by the transaction made through their mutual friend de Monfreid, whose sensitive portrait in oils of Fritz bending over the keyboard composing suggests how at ease Fritz was with artists. *Nevermore* was to be his most cherished possession for a quarter of a century.

The legacy further enabled him to give a concert entirely of his own music in London in the following year. Not a note of the lengthy programme had been heard in England before:

PART I

1. Fantasia for orchestra *Over the Hills and Far Away*
2. Légende for violin and orchestra
   (Solo violin: Mr. John Dunn)
3. Third and Fourth movements from Suite for orchestra *Folkeraadet*
4. Danish Songs (with orchestral accompaniment)

   'Through long, long years'
   'Let springtime come, then'
   Irmelin Rose
   ·On the seashore
   Wine roses

5. Symphonic poem for orchestra *The Dance Goes On*
6. *Mitternachtslied* (From Nietzsche's *Zarathustra*)
   For baritone solo, men's chorus and orchestra

PART II

Excerpts from *Koanga* (Opera in 3 acts with a prologue and epilogue)
1. (a) Prelude to Act III
   (b) Quintet and Finale of Act I
2. Act II

Critical reaction in the press was more favourable than unfavourable but no immediate impact was made. Fritz had to wait eight years at least before any conductor or organization showed further interest in his work. The concert—to quote Sir Thomas Beecham—'so far as England was concerned, might never have taken place!'

VI

The Quest

A glance at a list of musical works that Delius had completed by the end of the century would suffice to reveal the extent of his industry; operas, tone-poems and suites for orchestra, songs, chamber music and a concerto. And what, one may ask, does it all amount to? Vast reams of manuscript-paper covered with thousands upon thousands of notes, each representing a technical decision of mind, ear, eye (yes, and heart!) through countless hours with ruler and pen, and even more hours of meditation kept up steadily for years on end, and all in the quest of an intangible poetry which as yet had somehow eluded him! The thought is too cruel to contemplate: but it is near the truth, I think.

It is useless to deplore his late development or to compare his slow progress during these years with the assuredness at the same age of many of his other illustrious contemporaries; it was in the nature of the man to go his own way with a certain dogged obstinacy; there are passages in most of these early works which could not have been written by any one else. What is not clear throughout this stage is what he hoped to achieve ultimately by selecting the particular procedures he did and excluding others he felt to be useless. Was there some dawning of things to come in his gropings towards his later textures which were to owe so little to traditional practice?

Much of this formative work involved words. Fritz had wasted promising music on feeble libretti concocted by himself in *Irmelin* and *The Magic Fountain*. His sense of flow—geared to a Wagnerian slowness of pace and often propelled by Wagner's habit of leaning on the second beat of a bar—inclined to a more positive inventiveness in these operas, even though it was mainly derivative, than in the companion works for orchestra. The patterns

♫♩ ♩ (*Tristan and Isolde*) and ♫♩. ♪♫ (*Götterdämmerung*) sometimes maintain whole pages of music:

The Quest

Interlude from *Paa Vidderne* (Ibsen)

Without the impetus of words he was apt to build like a musical bricklayer in section upon section as with brick upon brick without the smoothness of real transition implicit in the lyrical style. One can feel the jolt at the asterisk in the extract from *Paa Vidderne*.

Up to 1899 when he sketched the first draft of his nocturne *Paris*, his long and arduous apprenticeship progressed in tiny advances in musicianship through working the same vein of lyrical material or reworking such passages as pleased him most and which, on pondering, he could realize to more purpose. Play this quotation from *Hiawatha* and feel its utter rigidity of movement which is even more so in the orchestral original through its note-for-note doubling of woodwind and strings:

The Quest

A theme from *Hiawatha*

Now play the same passage reworked later in *Paris* and feel its greater fluidity of movement and the freer flow of the individual parts and the relaxed subtlety of its harmonies:

Theme from *Paris* (*The Song of a Great City*)

Try and make the music sing through your fingers. Given Delius's imaginative scoring and flighted with insight and artistry in performance, this viola melody becomes a gesture—like opening a magic window to Innocence. Sir Thomas Beecham to whom I made this remark after one of his most felicitous renderings understood clearly what I meant in a quality which delighted him in Schubert. Delius was not to repeat this gesture anywhere else in his music. This suggestion of Innocence is rare in music and would have been lost completely in this instance had Delius given this melody to the first violins instead. Like Handel he was endowed with an uncanny knack of making his music sound well. Its clumsy appearance on paper comes from his vivid feeling for orchestral sounds regardless of their separate behaviour as integral parts of musical design. It is known that his music needs careful editing, yet he can seldom be faulted in the placing of sounds though some of his finest total effects provide the most awkward moments for his performers.

It is touching to trace in these early scores the painful progression from competence to mastery, or the deepening refinement that comes to first thoughts when reworked in a different musical context:

From *Scènes Parisiennes*

becomes

A passage from *Paris*

A curious feature of Delius's music is his growing obsession with a melodic figure based on the formula (though Fritz can never have thought of it as such):

a step upwards followed by *an upward leap*
a step downwards followed by *a downward leap*
followed by *a step downwards*:

The Quest

The Dance Goes On (1899)

Life's Dance (1901)

Paris (1899)

Paris

The Dark Fiddler's theme from *A Village Romeo and Juliet* (1900–1)

Elgar uses the same *motif* at the opening of his Violin Concerto:

Op. 61 (1910)

whereas Delius tends to associate it more with emotionally charged moments in the course of a work:

Sea-Drift (1903)

hei - sern Brül - len des Mee - - - res, o - der flat - ternd von
hoarse ___ sur - ging of the sea, ___ or flit - ting from

Busch zu Busch, bei Ta - - ge, hört' ich und sah
bri - er to bri - er by day, ___ I saw, I heard

10

im - mer wie - der den Ver - lass - - nen, ihn, den
at in - ter - vals the re - main - ing one, the

Eng. Hn.

Str. *p espressivo*   *fp*   3

Vo - - gel, den ein - sa - men Gast aus
he - - bird, the so - li - ta - ry guest from

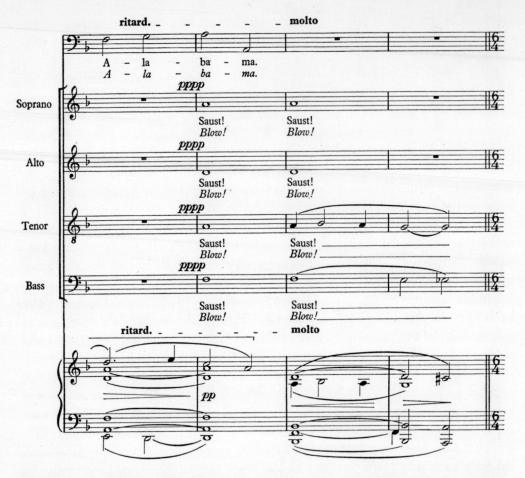

The change of orchestration at the double bar during the singing of the word 'heard' is a revealing touch of artistry in the sudden warmth of string tone at the telling cor anglais variant of the *motif* over the heaving wave-like basses. Such insights, one need hardly add, were, as yet, rare in the music he had written.

Fruition came in his formative period when he returned to France from his first London concert. The actual sounds of his orchestral invention had fired his imagination afresh and cleared up so many technical problems that he could scarcely wait to get back home to his unfinished manuscript *Paris*. The best of his unfledged works for orchestra aspired to a mastery then in vogue; of the handful of scores he possessed at Grez, half were by Richard Strauss. From Strauss he had learnt how to balance great forces and construct on an extended time-scale. To apply these techinques to his own designs was solely his *own* concern and so too was his sense of flow. The vast

German orchestras of the day were a challenge, and the expectations of his conductor friends Dr. Hans Haym and Fritz Cassirer were fulfilled undoubtedly in the new work.

Paris (*The Song of a Great City*)—a Nocturne—was the climax of his formative period: it also marked a personal crisis. Reluctantly he had come to realize he would never achieve what was in him to do unless he changed his way of life; this seemed impossible by staying in Paris. There was more to his turning up at Grez than the apparent main attraction, Jelka. The break, however, was not complete. Long after settling at Grez-sur-Loing he was always hankering in moments of leisure for his gayer companions in Montparnasse: too often, despite Jelka's rebukes, he was lured to his old haunts for days on end. The city had given him the friendships of artists; some, like Munch's, were to last a lifetime. At deeper levels were indelible memories of the natural beauties of her moods. These, on reflection, brought forth the music.

Delius subdues his orchestral colours in seeking to evoke the spirit of night brooding over the sleeping metropolis. The mellower timbres of clarinets and bassoons, violas and cellos combine in half-light shadings of tone reminiscent of the Dutch landscapist Jongkind's calm vistas of the city. Paris street-cries, now forgotten, reach the ear as from afar in rhythmic subtleties unique in his music. There are progressions in *Paris* which even today retain their novelty for discerning ears. Delius inscribed it to Dr. Haym who gave the first performance in Elberfeld in 1901; seven years later Mr. Thomas Beecham conducted it in London, since when it has appeared consistently in concert programmes throughout the world except, curiously, in the city of its origin.

Delius had studied Wagner for continuity, Chopin and Grieg as antidotes to pedantry and Strauss for orchestral fluency. Yet not until he found his *idea* (or more probably the *idea* found him!) did he also wholly find *himself*. It must have seemed to Cassirer and Haym that the qualities peculiar to this virile work were certain pointers to his future: but *Paris* could give them barely a hint of what we now know as the 'Delius sound'.

The work on which he was now engaged—*A Village Romeo and Juliet*—was to prove not only an original among operas but different from anything he had previously written. How it happened is a mystery. Maybe his closest friend 'B.G.' was right: that the malady he had caught in the pursuit of pleasure and was now apparently lying dormant was not unconnected with that wonder. Be that as it may. The *idea* we entangle with his maturest art produced a legacy of loveliness in music unsurpassed by any composer.

47

VII

The Great Noontide

There are two axioms by two French painters which are particularly relevant to Delius; one is by Braque, the other by Delacroix; both have bearing on his subsequent development.

'Progress in Art,' Braque reflected, 'does not consist of extension but in *knowledge of limits*.' Whatever the inner compulsion of spirit that transformed him into a composer of genius, the sequence of works that Delius wrote in the first decade of the new century can truly be called (in the words of Nietzsche) his *great noontide*. Delius became the artist he was from a knowledge of the limits of his latent powers plus a knowledge of the 'limits' the nature of those powers would impose on content and form. He recoiled, for instance, from symphony because he was temperamentally unsuited. He disliked intensely in all symphonies the stuff that comes between the tunes; the moment the intellect took over in any type of thematic development he had no further interest in the music. What he could have put in place of development, even had he treated it episodically as Mozart and others have occasionally done, would have been out of keeping with its style. He knew that the source of his lyrical artistry was intuitive, instinctive and warmed by the heart not by devices of the head.

Braque's axiom derives from Delacroix: 'What makes men of genius,' said Delacroix, 'or rather, what they make is not new ideas; it is the idea which obsesses them, that what has been said has still not been said enough.' Delius is one of the few composers to whom this dictum would apply outright. The themes that were to obsess him initially are as old as humanity itself; the sadness of partings, the briefness of love.

Foretastes of his mature idiom already occur in isolation in innumerable works in western music, and in none with more acuity than the madrigals of the early seventeenth-century Italian, Carlo Gesualdo, a remarkable character who tended to Delius's spiritual outlook. Words like *love, sorrow, death* were the main-springs of his musical invention. He points them in searing chromatic outbursts juxtaposed between words like *joy* in rapid, diatonic

Advertising the première of *Appalachia* outside Queen's Hall, London, in 1907

Below, the mountain region in Norway where Delius lived

A view from the garden of the composer's house, Grez-sur-Loing

Below, a street in the village

contrapuntal passages. *Diatonic* means music based solely on the related tones and half-tones of the scale in which the passage is written, whereas *chromatic* means adding extra half-tones outside that scale. 'Contrapuntal' implies a texture of musical phrases imitating each other in harmony at different times and at different levels. This apposition in differing tensions of diatonic and chromatic elements becomes a feature of Delius's style as it flowers under pressure of the *idea*.

Wagner in *Tristan and Isolde* had showed him the way to continuity in *A Village Romeo and Juliet* which he wrote in 1900–1. Its first production was conducted by Cassirer at the Komischer Oper in Berlin. That was in 1907 and Beecham followed three years later with performances in London. The libretto is based on a simple tale from Gottfried Keller's *People of Seldwyla*. It has features similar to Shakespeare's play, but instead of a feud between families of aristocrats there is ruinous strife between neighbouring farmers over an unclaimed strip of land. The rightful heir is a nameless vagabond, the Dark Fiddler, who haunts his land but never demands it. The real drama is the frustrated love of Sali and Vrenchen, the boy and girl of the rival farmers, a tragedy of the spirit rather than of incident expressed in essence in a moving interlude *The Walk to the Paradise Garden*. Delius, acting on Beecham's suggestion, prolonged the original to its present form in the last scene for the London production. The figure ♪♪♪ ♩ ♩|♩ is now absorbed into his musical blood stream leaving no trace of Wagnerian injection; the unmistakable flow of sound is immediately recognizable as his, Delius's, and his alone:

The Walk to the Paradise Garden

[Delius's directions:]
    Sali and Vrenchen are seen, thro' a veil
    on their way to the Paradise Garden   they stop and their
                                             lips meet in a long kiss

Vorhang auf. Man sieht SALI und VRENCHEN Hand in Hand nach dem Paradiesgarten wandern.
Curtain. SALI and VRELI are seen hand in hand on their way to the Paradise Garden.

D   49

Sie setzen sich ein Weilchen auf das Moos.
They sit down a little while on the moss.

SALI schließt VRENCHEN in seine Arme und küßt sie lang und innig.
SALI takes VRELI in his arms and kisses her long and tenderly.

Fritz was very hard up in 1902. There were no royalties to sustain him whilst he worked: only the chance of possible performances usually in promises that came to nothing. He wrote an opera *Margot-la-Rouge* and entered it for a competition for which Ravel provided the piano reduction, but it left him not one franc the richer. Exhausted temporarily by constant composing he relaxed over sketches for *Appalachia* begun somewhat feebly for orchestra in 1895. The title is misleading. Delius meant it to apply to the whole of North America; including the Mississippi River, whereas, geographically, Appalachia refers to a specific region running from Pennsylvania to Alabama. These sketches were based on a tune he had heard sung by Negroes in tobacco stemmeries in Danville, Virginia, as they ripped the veins out of tobacco leaves before the days of automation. Fritz was soon ripe to exploit another facet of the *idea*. Thus *Appalachia*, a set of variations on this old Negro slave-song; it reveals the measure of his detachment from trends in contemporary composition and his self-centredness as an artist; it has been preferred by some to his later work.

A sprawling orchestral introduction evokes the Mississippi landscape and the affectionate humour of the Negro population employed on the plantations by the river banks. The tune is then heard first from the cor anglais and comes and goes imaginatively with brief whispered choral responses; its emotional peak is reached in the doggerel of a beautiful variation for unaccompanied chorus, *After night has gone comes the day*:

Variation from *Appalachia* for unaccompanied chorus

The Great Noontide

This is followed by the most imaginative nature-music he had yet written and so obviously inspired by his American experiences. The river heaving lazily, the mystery of the woods, the 'sweltering heat'—one can feel, even see their image in this music:

The second variation from *Appalachia*

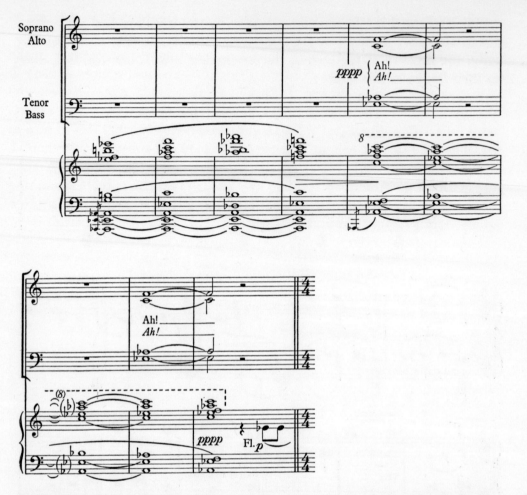

A baritone solo *Oh Honey, I'm going down the river in the morning* leads to a joyous epilogue; the slaves link their longing for their lost loved ones to the destiny of the mighty river.

America had been an exciting influence, but disturbing nevertheless; it had enlarged his mind, deepened his intuition and satisfied a natural inquisitiveness about American Negro culture. *Appalachia* is a big conception in the spread of its panoramic nature music on a scale befitting its subject. His early works had been full of tunefulness but usually little else. To convey ideas of grandeur and mystery solely by tunefulness rarely accords with the basic problem of filling a big canvas of transitional designs. The melodic variations are a delight; the harmonic variations are peculiarly personal. Here he relies with a craftsman's skill on varying the degrees of chromatic departure from the focal key-centre of each variation; the treatment is

54

subtle in nuance of feeling from one variation to another and in relation to the whole.

One of the melodic variations, however, seems slightly out of place in the scheme as though by some chance an English scene had somehow merged into the American landscape. It is then in an episode removed from the theme that the miracle happened, I believe, and despite his recent experience in *A Village Romeo and Juliet* Delius divined clearly what was in him to do. The clue to that insight is here, in my view, in this strange, ethereal, visionary passage ruminating on the rim of mystery like the moss veiling the forests of the American South. These few bars express in truth something beyond the evocation of nature, not new ideas, but *the idea*; the transitoriness of all mortal things mirrored in Nature:

An orchestral episode from *Appalachia*

From now on, instead of such single passages, entire works were to be prompted by this obsession, and the *idea* becomes caught up characteristically even in his purely orchestral music. It colours eventually all he wrote, illumined often unforgettably by rays of musical poetry the more striking perhaps by the apparent monotony of his inspiration.

The best-known choral work in this *genre* is *Sea-Drift*, composed in 1903 and first performed at Essen in Germany in 1906. It is a setting for baritone, chorus and orchestra of words selected from Walt Whitman's *Out of the Cradle Endlessly Rocking* from his anthology of poems *Leaves of Grass*. A young bird-watcher by the sea, the she-bird that never returns, the he-bird's cries for its mate, and the boy's share in its grief—these every-day experiences Delius pondered and transmuted into emotional lyrical music symbolizing the boy's awakening to the mystery of separation and death. The soloist identifies himself in turn with the boy-narrator and the anguished bird; the chorus intensifies the drama by sharing the narrative or re-echoing poignant lines in the text.

The poem might have been specially written for Delius; its lyrical conception of the *idea* is appealing; the words and their emotional overtones are imaginatively apt for the 'Delius sound'; their arrangement invites a vocal line of irregular angularity—a kind of musical poetic-prose—such as he had been striving to achieve through the action of four operas. Nowhere in these does he attain such felicities as in the solo line in *Sea-Drift*. His pointing of phrase at *with bright eyes* when describing the silent 'she-bird crouch'd on her nest', for instance, or, *wonderful, causing tears* when the he-bird sits 'all night long on a moss-scalloped stake down almost amid the slapping waves' is as inevitable and memorable as anything in Schubert.

Sea-Drift was introduced to English audiences by Sir Henry Wood at the Sheffield Festival of 1908 and established itself through subsequent performances as one of the great choral masterpieces of this century.

An event in September of 1903 caused Fritz to write at once to Grieg: '. . . On the 25th I married my friend Jelka Rosen here in Grez (of course a civil ceremony). I have got even further away from God and Jesus. We lived together in "wild marriage" for six years but we found it more practical to legalise our relationship—get everything cheaper—and one gets free and without further ado a certificate of honesty and good manners. If you go to Germany next winter please let me know for I have several performances and should like very much to introduce my wife to you and Frau Grieg—she's a painter and very gifted—and then I should also very much like you to hear my music—you only know my first attempts—unfortunately I can't send you anything for I have not yet found a publisher—although I must say I have not tried very much—and I am writing exclusively orchestral music—every year I have three or four performances in Germany—Buths at Dusseldorf and Dr. Haym in Elberfeld produce my latest scores every year. . . . My *Mitternachtslied* I don't need to tell you has absolutely no relationship whatever with Strauss's *Zarathustra* which I consider a complete failure. But I find *Till Eulenspiegel* and *Heldenleben* are quite marvellous works. *Tod und Verklärung* I find not so significant although there is much that is beautiful in it. There is too much Liszt and Berlioz—I think he will do best in humouristic items . . . I greet you and your dear wife most heartily and remain in old affection,

> Your
> Frederick Delius
> (my new name!)

Delius, following Nietzsche, had renounced the Christian code of ethics although he did not subscribe entirely to all Nietzsche's tenets. To tell the truth at all costs; courage to live fearlessly—to say 'Yea' in the face of all that in his judgment cramps the human spirit on its brief, meaningless life on earth; then, still more, courage to die fearlessly—that was the supreme achievement of man.

Two years (1904–5) were spent in the composition of a paean to the Will which embodies these ideals, *A Mass of Life,* the grandest of Delius's choral works. The title suggests a unique non-conformity. The text which Cassirer helped him to select from Nietzsche's *Thus Spake Zarathustra* is biblical in style; poetry, metaphor and irony blending in a revelation of Nietzsche's gospel of the Eternal Recurrence. It is not easy to convey coherently the precise meaning of the often seemingly extravagant sayings that Nietzsche puts into the mouth of his superman Zarathustra. Delius, though a man after Nietzsche's heart, produced his masterpiece by concentrating on the poetic fragments he felt were most apt to the full expression of his musical symbols rather than by attempting deliberately to disseminate philosophical ideas. Four soloists, large choral and orchestral forces are employed in typically Delian manner in a sequence of eleven soliloquies in two parts; the singers share the words of Zarathustra, personified in the baritone soloist, now declaiming, now meditating, now mingling dynamically as human instruments in the orchestral texture. Zarathustra's *Night-Song* (*Mitternachtslied*, to which reference has already been made) crowns the work in a descant of Joy which craves 'eternal, endless day!' *A Mass of*

Life occurs like a vast parentheses in the progression of Delius's works, unlike any other, but necessary to his development. The first complete performance of the *Mass* was directed by Beecham in London in June 1909.

Balfour Gardiner, the English composer, provided Delius with suitable material for the other choral work of this period which expresses the *idea* in another perspective—the transience of creaturely love, its partings, frailties and separations reflected in Nature's autumnal twilights. Gardiner had sent him a copy of verse by Ernest Dowson, the English poet, who ran to seed in the cafés of Dieppe; by gleaning carefully from these poems he devised a song-cycle *Songs of Sunset*.

Dowson is out of fashion these days but his poetry lives in *Songs of Sunset* through the shafts of Delius's musical poetry which penetrate the verbal imagery to a purely musical idea of the mood. It can be 'heard' in the singular quality of the sound even without the use of words. Delius's haunting musical symbols impose their own restraints on his textures in sustaining the mood throughout the movements. One such symbol, a plaintive phrase (lah soh lah, me, at its earliest appearance) yields melodically to emotional changes and virtually holds the work together. Chorus and soloists sing in turn of the day that is 'almost done' for lovers, of the weariness of love that can never bloom again; a choral epilogue *They are not long the days of wine and roses* fades characteristically 'within a dream'. Beecham, who was very fond of this piece, gave it first at a Delius concert at Queen's Hall in London in 1911.

Another friend, Percy Grainger, fired Delius's imagination by sending him his own choral setting of a folksong *Brigg Fair*; he had taken it down from an old man's singing whilst on a visit to Lincolnshire. Delius, he urged, was the one composer who could write the kind of orchestral variations for which the tune cried out! So following a period of prodigious work in large-scale forms of his own contriving Delius was compelled to centre his mind in the frame of an English folksong and project it on a smaller time-scale than in his previous variations *Appalachia*. The verses run:

> *It was the fift' of August*
> *The weather fine and fair*
> *Unto Brigg Fair I did repair*
> *For love I was inclined.*
>
> *I rose up with the lark in the morning*
> *With my heart so full of glee*

Of thinking there to meet my dear
Long time I wished to see.

The green leaves they shall wither
And the branches they shall die
If ever I prove false to her
To the girl that loves me.

Brigg Fair: a Choral arrangement by Percy Grainger

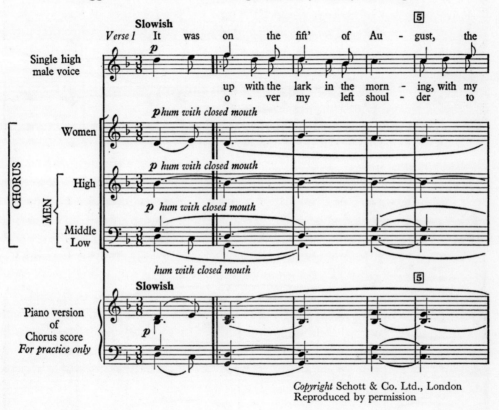

Brigg Fair: theme and first variation by Delius

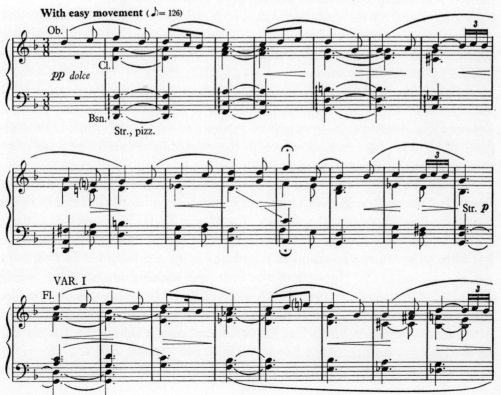

VAR. II

Str. *mp*

Play the two versions and feel the greater contrast in Delius's setting between the diatonic and chromatic harmonies in the opening bars. Note, too, how Grainger spoils the effect in bar 6 by returning to the G minor chord heard in bar 3; whereas Delius, by the element of surprise, becomes magical at once in the unexpectedness of the G major chord. Now play the first variation introduced by the flute with its wonderful sense of gradual awakening to the glorious scope of riches to come. This downward chromatic slithering of harmonies in the hands of mediocrity would be unbearable. Every progression gives a hint to the course of its possible resolution but contains these essential elements of surprise. Notice how the drift is in similar motion until the approach to the apex of the tune when it blossoms in contrary motion between the outer parts—a touch of instinctive technique within the confines of his style—to push on through the exceptional interrupted cadence (exceptional at this stage) to the next variation.

As usual Delius goes his own way; an evocative introduction, the folksong from the oboe with woodwind accompaniment, repetitions that call to mind the early English manner of Byrd's *The Woods So Wild* (though doubtless Delius had never heard of it); a beautiful meditation unmindful of the tune but akin to it; more variations in which the reins are loosened in rhapsody and finally, after the clamour of the Fair, the melting music of the lovers mirrored in tranquil Nature. The harmonic and rhythmic changes on the tune ring 'like varying aspects of the same type of countryside'. Delius was never more English in his feeling for orchestral colour than here. Rarely has he used the dry timbres of the bass clarinet to more telling effect.

In the spring of the following year, 1908, he wrote a musical impression of his garden at Grez. His reverie induced eventually a masterpiece of orchestral fantasy (for he revised it drastically after the first performance in 1909)— *In a Summer Garden*. Delius's house stood on the village street between the old church and a ruined keep, the high stone walls of his garden sloping down beyond the orchard to the river. He must often have longed for the summer change of a landscape that is swamp-like from autumn to spring, but in summer the white courtyard was ablaze with flowers and his little world was closed in by the great trees at the water's edge. Indoors, apart from works by Gauguin and Munch, all the paintings on the walls revealed colourful studies of the garden in summer painted, of course, by Jelka. But the garden itself was her masterpiece, and the musical imagery it worked in Delius's mind was fittingly dedicated to her.

The texture of the score, despite its full forces, has the quality of chamber music and suggests with infinite subtlety the sounds and colours of the scene. It opens quietly in chant-like tones for wind quintet, echoed in the strings with a flitting figure from the oboe. To hear this and no more, we are caught up into the composer's dream. In listening to this work by gramophone memorise the rhythm of that flitting figure, for it, not the opening phrase, is the leaven of much of the musical action. The development of its salient rhythmic details is as masterly as its melodic shaping. For instance, the rhythm at the peak of the flute phrase (following immediately upon the oboe at the beginning of the work) expands in joyous outburst at the first entry of the full orchestra. There is more artifice in this man's music than is ever conceded; it never boasts itself but mingles naturally in its flow. Delius is rarely given credit for the new type of prose-melody he invented, geared to tensions of chromatic stress. In this work the line is firm, clear and lyrical as in song. A more spacious singing comes in the middle section from the violas; then as the current of the passing river deepens, horn and trumpet join in turn to the murmuring of the woodwind. We leave the water-lilies and the giant poplars as the more animated music of the garden swells in rapturous ascendancy. Gradually the exultant mood relaxes in tranquillity, the opening phrase is heard in the strings and after moments of yearning and reluctance the vision of the garden fades as the dragon-flies dart over the pond.

Different again in character and action from *Appalachia* and *Brigg Fair* is another set of variations for orchestra—*Dance Rhapsody No. 1* which he wrote in 1908 and conducted the first performance of at the Three Choirs Festival at Hereford in September of the following year, one of the few occasions on which he was persuaded to direct his music. He recalled the event with mixed feelings—'I had little talent for conducting and, to make matters worse, I caught a severe chill and had my wallet stolen just before the concert!'

Reaction to Delius when he dances (and like Zarathustra he was prone to dance) depends on whether his dancing appeals; whether one cares for his rhythmic foot-falls and whether his rhythms take flight in one's mind; whether to some the 'Delius sound' seems alien to the measures of dance. He is easy to follow when he changes step though his perambulations are apt to be clumsy. And if his dancing is not to one's taste one can always sit out the penultimate variation when he ceases his dancing for a while and listen to the tune in the solo violin above ravishing harmonies in muted strings. Sir Henry Wood confessed to me that he had never conducted this variation unmoved.

No work by Delius is more neglected than that which ends this great decade, the opera *Fennimore and Gerda*. It is a country tale of frustrated love contemporary with the time of its composition (1908–10) and based on a novel *Niels Lyhne* by the Danish writer Jens Peter Jacobsen. Delius's aim was a short, sharp opera—it lasts but ninety minutes in all—in which to project the *idea* afresh: the futility of striving for happiness in passion intensified here by interaction with the artistic disillusionments of the two men in the triangle, Niels, a young poet, and Erik, a painter. Nothing could be farther from the ways of grand opera than the tragedy of these ordinary people made pathetically insignificant by reflection in Delius's musical imagery of Autumn's dying beauties. Niels is in love with Fennimore, Erik's wife, whilst Erik, bored with country life, goes to pieces in the city. Fennimore and Niels then declare their love but she rejects him with remorse when she learns that Erik has been killed in an accident. Three years pass and Niels, now a farmer, proposes to and is accepted by a teenager, Gerda.

The opera is divided into eleven mood-pictures with pauses to mark the passage of time. Producer and conductor must be at one in their conception of the work to avoid an effect of fragmentation. Each picture is a separate musical movement developed with terse economy of means in textures original in colour and design. This is the most Delian work to date; not a bar could have been written by anyone else. Yet the melodic thread throughout each picture woos the ear but does not win it with the memorable felicities one might have expected in Delius's solo vocal lines. But the orchestral sound of this remarkable score anticipates in many passages the unmixed timbres of works like *Summer Night on the River* on which his fame may ultimately rest. He had to wait until after World War I for the first

The old bridge at Grez-sur-Loing

Below, the view from the bridge of Delius's meadow in the early morning

Delius, his wife and Percy Grainger in the summer of 1923
Below, the composer at his piano. Directly behind him is Jelka's copy of Gauguin's painting, *Nevermore*; Delius had sold the original in 1920

performance of the opera at Frankfurt in 1919. Delius was well satisfied with its reception.

The great noontide had passed: but the day was to have a long evening!

VIII

The Long Evening

'My works have been the most important events in my life.' By now they had become equally so with Jelka who was beginning to abandon her painting to translate his operas, choral works and songs. In 1911 Delius was making preliminary sketches for another choral work *An Arabesque* again to words by Jacobsen and also *A Song of the High Hills* for wordless choir and orchestra. He was to finish, however, a miniature tone-poem unique in all his music in its sense of depicting as well as evoking the spirit of the scene—*Summer Night on the River*. Moments in the forest scene in Act III of *Koanga* and again in *Appalachia* have strong visual suggestiveness but these are less sustained. Listening to *Summer Night on the River* one can almost see the gnats and dragonflies darting over the water-lilies and the faint white mist hovering over the willow-tressed banks and overhanging trees. Here Delius's imagination leads him to an orchestral pointillism rare in his nature–music but saved from mere artifice by its dependence on melody. Sir Thomas Beecham always maintained that this was the most searching piece by Delius to realize with vision in performance.

Delius contrived whenever possible to spend his summers in Norway. This was his spiritual home where the best of his works were pondered, often through weeks of silence even when Jelka was there, to be written down later in France. Such was his tireless energy that before he took a cottage overlooking the hills he usually walked and climbed alone; occasionally Jelka went with him and once the then 'Mr' Beecham also, whom he never forgave for forgetting his sandwiches the day they lunched on a glacier!

He recalled his fiftieth year when he was compelled to remain in Grez: '*The Song of the High Hills* was not going well. Passages eluded me; one in particular, the eight-part chorus that wouldn't come right!' He remarked, too, that this was the only occasion on which he had not been able to bring himself to put a work aside. In no other work does Delius convey the sense of 'wide open spaces' more imaginatively. Through the sparing use of his wordless chorus he extends the spiritual range of his forces and fuses his orchestral and human voices in a blend of musical nature-worship which, in this most personal context, symbolizes his flight in sound. We set out in good heart till the pace slows before the immensities of peak and cloud in the growing orchestral rapture of the hill-song. Then through cooler heights of mist and snow we climb to fuller sublimity. A myriad of voices merge from afar till the grandeur of Nature is matched in song: another of Sir Henry Wood's spine-chilling moments! We begin the descent the way we came still musing on life and its mystery. Eight years were to pass before the new piece was first performed by Albert Coates with the Philharmonic Choir at a concert of the Royal Philharmonic Society in London.

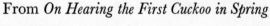

From *On Hearing the First Cuckoo in Spring*

From *I Ola-Dalom, i Ola-Kjønn*   (Grieg)

Ped. sempre al Fine

Seldom does the best-known work by a composer contain his most charac-
teristic utterance; seldom still to find that work purely contemplative of
natural things as in Delius's evocative idyll for small orchestra *On Hearing the
First Cuckoo in Spring* composed the same year as *The Song of the High Hills*
and first given by Mengelberg at another Philharmonic concert in London
in 1914. The brief introduction is a master-stroke, an epitome in itself of
Delius's mature art. Whenever heard, if conducted with insight, it captures
in felicity his sense of the awakening countryside in Spring, 'a world of
memory in one mournful chord, a world of thought in one translucent
phrase'. For to Delius, musing on the Norwegian folksong on which his
music is based, it is plain to hear that, even though it is of Spring that he
sings 'there is a world of sorrow in one little song'. Not oppressive, but a sweet
sadness and the cuckoo notes on the clarinet (in the middle section) do not
depict so much as kindle afresh that yearly youthful delight which none of
us outgrow. A comparison with Grieg's piano-piece, to which Delius is not
a little indebted, will reveal the extent he had pushed his chromaticism far
beyond anything Grieg would have dared. In this and *Summer Night on the
River* their magical sounds are conjured up with less than the complement
of Mozart's orchestra! In the best of Delius we are made one with Nature.
No man has given music to all her moods, but in the expression of her tran-
quillities he excelled all others.

Another Nature work, *North Country Sketches*, dedicated to Albert Coates,
was completed in 1914 but was introduced by Sir Thomas Beecham with the
London Symphony Orchestra at a London concert in 1915. It is Delius's
one instrumental work in which he recalls expressly his impressions of the
Yorkshire countryside he had known as a boy, though it may be of interest
to add that years later before dictating a new opening to *A Song of Summer* in
his garden in France he told me to imagine we were sitting among the
heather on the Yorkshire moors by the sea.

The orchestral colours of these musical symbols of our wilder northern

70

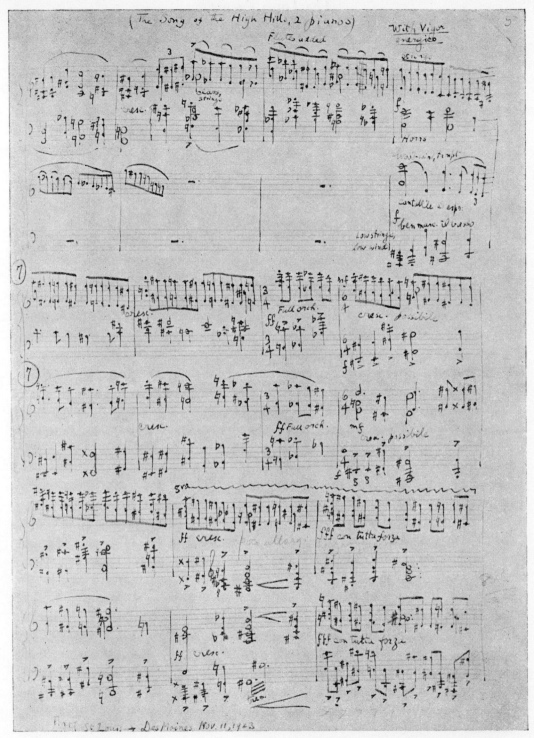

Percy Grainger's manuscript arrangement of *The Song of the High Hills*, 1923

moorland landscape have sharper, more bracing qualities of timbre than those that are to be heard in *Brigg Fair,* for instance, which Delius placed much further south than Lincolnshire in his music. There is more pictorial suggestion than is usual in Delius in the first two movements despite his nature titles. The division of strings into twelve parts, the imaginative pre-occupation with texture (rather than tune), the astringent harmonies drooping in motion, the lyrical oboe all but silent, now joined by two others in bleak figurations with icy fingerings from the harps call up the visual winter landscape whilst cellos, horn, then clarinets and bassoons lament the lifeless scene.

Delius is not easy on his performers; the right sense of colour and weight on the note in the right place for the instrumentalist. A flexible hand, firm yet unprejudiced, a flair for balancing the singing phrase from the conductor; a helping hand, too, in dance movements when Delius, resisting modulation, and defying the laws of musical gravity expects to maintain dance-like motion from phrases made static by often ending exactly where they began. *The March of Spring,* light and lively, throbs rhythmically in hope of the *Summer Garden* through quiet ruminatings to joyous outburst culminating in the march-like tune which gradually dies in the distance—the most difficult movement to bring off technically in all his orchestral music.

Delius completed *An Arabesque* whilst staying at Sir Thomas Beecham's house outside Watford in 1915. He and Jelka had fled from Grez before the German advance; they were awaiting permission to cross the North Sea from Newcastle to Bergen and remain in Norway at their cottage until the end of the war. Jacobsen's poem is a strange phantasy in which passion is personified in the God Pan; a lover's rhapsody on the briefness of bliss. Jacobsen, a botanist, was a true countryman, whose translation of Darwin's *Origin of Species* won him far greater fame than his poetry.

There is power here in Delius's music and to spare; an effortless virtuosity in deploying his voices and orchestra in a refined and masterly means of expression. The opening sounds, reminiscent of the last movement of the first violin sonata (begun in 1905 and finished in 1915), rise mysteriously from the depths in divided violas and cellos to flower in a descending sequential figure in the violins which plays an important expressive role in the eventual course of the music. Delius delights in woodwind arabesques and maintains independent divided strings in great freedom throughout, so that the chorus has its own autonomous life and breaks the convention that the chorus basses in the texture must double the orchestral basses. The same size orchestra is made to produce richer sonorities in more copious designs than those of the more intimate *Songs of Sunset*, whilst the role of the chorus is reduced to effective commentaries on or re-echoings of the sentiments expressed by the baritone soloist. Yet Delius never surpassed its spellbound final pages, a musical image of the death of love mirrored in the bleakness of a northern winter landscape. The first performance of this superb work was at Newport, Wales in 1920.

Delius was deeply seared by the wastage of youth in the carnage of the First World War. It involved him painfully in conflicting loyalties when relatives and the sons of friends faced each other as unwilling foes. His *Requiem—To the memory of all young artists fallen in the war* is not a requiem in the traditional sense as understood in Latin Christianity but Delius's own singularly personal lament for man's gullibility—the 'tale of falsehoods and golden visions', the 'house of lies' of religion as men of differing faiths cry in vain for God. It has taken another World War and a revolution in insights into the meaning and purpose of life to admit a more tolerant attitude to such notions. Man, he always insisted, is a mystery; Nature alone is eternally renewing. Thus predictably its finest pages are of an evocative beauty, notably in such passages as 'The snow lingers yet in the mountains'. Such moments as these invariably capture the imagination of music lovers all over the world. The *Requiem* stems from the *Arabesque* rather than from *Sea-Drift*. Delius's huge orchestral forces are disposed as never before in his music. Triple woodwind often sound in pairs, yet six horns are used with discrimination, more, for instance, than in *Brigg Fair*. He mixed his orchestral timbres where normally he prefers pure colour, and disposes his melodic strands, especially in the strings and brass, with telling sureness and skill. There is a harshness, too, in his harmonic thought from which he was later to recoil. The vocal lines of his soloists are again less memorable than in *Sea-Drift*, and the mystery of Delius will always remain that despite the asperities of his choral writing it is supremely imaginative in original sounds and often thrilling in effect. In no other work by Delius is his character as a man more clearly revealed—betrayed even—than in this curious *Requiem*.

Delius had more unfinished works than usual at this time. The war had made it impossible to concentrate for long; he had started a number of projects and left them to lie fallow. Jelka had strapped these manuscripts to her life-belt for fear of being torpedoed in the Channel and again on crossing over to Norway! Once settled there he took them up anew and completed *Dance Rhapsody (No. 2)*, *Eventyr*, a string quartet, a sonata for cello and piano, songs, two unaccompanied choruses *To be sung of a summer night on the water*, *A Song before Sunrise* for small orchestra, a concerto for violin, cello and orchestra and a violin concerto.

Eventyr is Delius's orchestral show-piece, his only work that suggests narrative whilst evoking the spirit of the scene. Appropriately it is set in Norway embodied in a collection of folk-tales of that name published in 1841 by Asbjörnsen and Moe. The musical interest turns on the play and interaction of two groups of themes; the one, in the strings, expressing the idea of the warmhearted superstitious peasantry in these tales; the other, in the woodwind and brass, the eerie interventions in their lives of the fantastic creatures of Norwegian legend—the trolls, giants, demons, pixies. Sir Henry Wood, to whom it is dedicated, gave the first performance in London in 1919.

Delius's most enduring achievements have been made as in *Sea-Drift*, *An Arabesque*, or *In a Summer Garden*, when personal idiosyncrasies of form and content have been satisfied intrinsically with the growth of each work. When, in attempting pieces styled 'Sonata' or 'Concerto'—the musical and formal implications of which are foreign to his very nature—he substitutes his own brand of continuity, he not only poses great problems for himself but invites strong criticism for his pains. By *his own* rather than traditional standards the violin concerto is regarded as the best, though Delius himself preferred his cello concerto composed in 1921. Two introductory expectant bars and the solo violin enters magnificently in unceasing song through bravura, meditation, accompanied cadenza and even dance to end in a cadence of Delian dreams. He obviously realized that certain types of thematic invention are indispensable in writing concertos. The orchestral reiterations of the opening theme in the violin concerto plainly reveal his feeling for the need of such repetitions in concerto. It is largely by making such concessions to the importance of contrasts (as in classical procedure) in the persistent fanfare motives in the brass that the violin concerto sounds more concerto-like than the cello or double concertos. Yet he was quite unaccountable. He ushers in the double concerto with a gesture of classical pretensions unequalled by any composer of his generation: but that is all we hear of it! Again, the stuff of the violin concerto attains more formal and thematic cohesion than the material of his other concertos. His prolonged dislike of his piano concerto was due not so much to weakness of form as embarrassment by its content. Lapses of taste were anathema to Delius!

Delius wrote about sixty songs altogether in five languages; Norwegian— in which, notwithstanding his upbringing, he was more proficient than in German; French—the sound of which he grew to detest and spoke very rarely when I knew him; Danish, German and English. He would often pause in a major task to set some lyric when its mood and feelings were akin to his own and suggested a musical poetry he was unable to resist. The exquisitely turned French songs are French in spirit, without affectation yet truly Delian. They were written at intervals between 1895 and 1919 and capture with unusual precision the now faded sentiments of that era. Distinct from these, the English songs, written at the persuasion of Lady Cunard at Watford in 1915–16, though fresh, charming and spontaneous, demand more lively and flexible treatment and are difficult to perform successfully for both singer and accompanist. The Celtic *I—Brasil*, perhaps Delius's most haunting song, evokes the sorrow on the wind calling us away to the legendary islands of peace.

After the war the Deliuses returned by way of Germany to Grez to find their home turned upside down. It had been taken over by the army authorities as an English officers' mess; 'they'd even pinched my fishing-rod, but they didn't get at the wine! We'd stacked logs over the cellar steps and they never discovered the door!' The war had played havoc with Delius's affairs; he had managed his investments with shrewdness and foresight but found that the copyrights of his works had been sold and resold in Germany and Austria. This was to involve him in litigation and constant worry for years to come; thereafter he avoided business with lawyers.

The situation was saved, however, by the appearance at Grez of Basil Dean who commissioned him to write the incidental music to Elroy Flecker's play *Hassan* which he proposed to stage in London. Delius immediately set to work and completed the score to Dean's requirements. Three years were to pass before Dean was ready. Meanwhile Delius was alarming his friends with the first signs of his approaching affliction. Dean then decided he needed more music and but for the presence of Percy Grainger who was staying with the Deliuses at their cottage in Norway (and who finished the orchestration as Delius was finding it difficult to hold his pen), the score would not have been delivered in time. With Henry Ainley as Hassan and Eugene Goossens conducting the small orchestra the production was a great success enhanced by the poetry of Delius's music.

Delius, fortunately, still could see and prepared for the publication of his second sonata for violin and piano, with Jelka's help as copyist. Though regarded primarily as a harmonist, his flights of melodic poetic-prose especially in the cello sonata aspire to a long-spanned freedom of phrase rare in British music. To sustain convincing flow of such melody even in a single line is still the most difficult feat, I think, in the trade of writing music.

The function of the piano in Delius's sonatas is mainly 'to load every rift with ore'; such chordal highlighting of the melodic line serves but to increase one's scrutiny. Delius succeeds where so many have failed.

And now began a depressing round of visits to German spas with Jelka in search of a cure.

IX

The Recluse of Grez

Four years of useless journeying brought no improvement in Delius's health. Due to syphilis he was becoming more and more emaciated; nothing that cures or doctors could do made any permanent impression. Eventually he lost his sight completely and his lower limbs became paralyzed. The best that Jelka could do for him now—for he loved routine—was to frame a new life round him at Grez. Not that it had been otherwise all along. She had always sacrificed her interests to his. Her devotion was constant almost obstinate, although he sometimes tried her near to tears. A strange, remote yet lovable quality prompted attachment from those about him; the cook who came in from the village daily; the Saxon house-maid who lived in; the seamstress, the gardener, the untidy young man who drove the old Ford on market days to Fontainebleau; even the male nurses from Germany on whom he depended utterly and who hated doing their stint at Grez were known to have periods of dedication.

This was his immediate world bounded by his garden when I joined him in the presumptuous hope of trying to help him to work again. I had been fired by his music on first hearing it early in 1928 and so distressed by the news of his plight in not being able to complete his life's work that I had written offering my services, if acceptable to him, as his amanuensis. Delius had dictated a letter inviting me to go to Grez to see if I liked it before deciding definitely. He warned me that he and his wife were much on their own and rarely had visitors. I was not put off by this; my mind was made up. I would go.

The first night I was initiated into a remarkable ritual to be repeated daily except when it rained. Delius was dressed in an Inverness cape; a French beret was clapped on his head and he was then carried to a push-cart standing in the porch. The great door to the street was opened and with a flickering oil-lamp to light the way he was trundled into the darkness by his goose-stepping nurse whilst Jelka and I took turns behind holding an umbrella to shield him from the wind. We proceeded in silence up the main street and out beyond the houses to the road which Jelka said led on to Marlotte, about three miles away. It was on this stretch of highway here that he had mused upon his finest works when not up in the hills of Norway. This he told me some months later. He was not given to talking about music. After a mile or so we came back still in silence to the house. The great door was closed and I bade them 'Good-night'; thus I became one of the household.

Frederick Delius was a rare spirit. Nothing about him was more unusual than his calm but curiously disturbing presence instantly discernible on approaching him and such as I have never experienced since in any other human being. His conversation gave no clue to a life committed to composition. He spoke his mind regardless of censure and could be withering in his contempt for erudition as the Professor of Music in the University of Cambridge, Edward Dent, was unlikely to forget. 'Dent! You're not musical any more! Too much learning!' Dent's retort was no less forthright: 'You heard what Delius said to me? Fenby! He's right!' Professor Dent had come to lunch to collect material for his book on Busoni, the German-Italian pianist-composer. Delius's reminiscences were laced with humour: 'At Busoni's we always sat on forms; there was Gerda and the dwarfs who were there for luck and a bevy of Busoni's adoring females. If possible I avoided sitting next to Sibelius although we always got on well. But he usually had had a drop too much, and his form used to tremble from end to end through all those great long-winded sonatas that Busoni used to play to us!'

Delius, apparently, was out of touch with the lot of the ordinary professional musician. He believed that music atrophied in the hands of the rank and file; this did more harm than good in preventing its wide appeal. He had suffered much in his early days through insensitive playing of his music. The great improvement in orchestral standards was very timely for him; Delius owes more to his players than almost any other composer. He was a perfectionist, too, to his finger-tips and loathed mediocrity. There were no half measures with Delius; he was always a man of extremes. He abhorred the whole system of musical training as fundamentally *unmusical* except in the teaching of instruments. He had little faith in men collectively unless they were playing in orchestras! He made no attempts, as far as I know, to secure performances of his works—though Jelka was always prodding Beecham. This, of course, was understandable, for together with caring for Delius, his music was now her chief concern. Delius seemed to embody for me all that is finest in Nietzsche's *Zarathustra* which had been his breviary throughout his manhood; his fearless attitude to life, superb independence, solitariness, his stoicism in suffering, his proud, stern, untameable spirit, his hardness, so unfathomable. These qualities were tempered by a certain charm, a dry wit, a boyish weakness for detective stories, a fastidious delight in the pleasures of the table, and a dandyish love of good clothes.

The question of Debussy's possible influence often arises in discussing Delius. It was put to Delius by Cassirer in 1904 when remarking on the 'enormous influence' Debussy appeared to have exercised on Delius in *A Village Romeo and Juliet*. 'You must tell me what your relations are to Debussy? . . . who is the teacher and who the pupil? We have no trace of Delius's reply, but from what I learnt from Alden Brooks, his neighbour and intimate friend for more than a quarter of a century, and who lived in the former priest's house on the other side of the garden wall, it seems that Delius's practical interest in Debussy's music was active only about the time of his writing *Summer Night on the River*. Delius had acquired a pianola and with his customary but usually short-lived excess had driven poor Brooks from his study to Paris by playing *L'Après-midi d'un faune* for hours on end with the windows open! He had written to Granville Bantock, the English composer, in February, 1908: 'Do you know that I have never in my life heard *L'après Midi d'un Faune* (sic) or seen the music.' The letter (p. 80) is interesting too in the 'slight alterations' Delius proposes to make to the score of *Brigg Fair*. (The 'incident' refers to the first performance of Holbrooke's *Apollo and the Seaman*, based on a poem by Herbert Trench, which Bantock had just heard in London. The critics had 'spotted that it was botched up from an earlier work *The Masque of the Red Death!*' The Musical League, incidentally, was a fruitless attempt to promote British music with Elgar and Delius as figureheads.)

The only reference I recall by Delius to Debussy's music was in the garden in 1930 (and that obliquely); he was deploring Gauguin's treatment of his wife together with Debussy's of his first wife 'Lily-Lilo'. 'I admire Debussy's refinement, his orchestration, his conceptions, but I find his harmony mannered and his music deficient in melody.'

Delius obviously knew what he was about and exactly what was going on in European music. After his early dependence on Wagner—he was incredibly slow to work through that influence—he cast his swiftly roving eye wherever his musical fancy pleased: but there was precious little that pleased him! With his detestation of German music, excluding certain works by Strauss, his disdain of British music in general ('Music is now in exactly the same state as painting was in France at the time of Manet,' he had

I found also Bell's piece interesting & honest - rather Wagnerian.

GREZ SUR LOING.
S. ET M.

My dear Bantock — Feb 1 1908

Your letter just received - I was very much amused by the Holbrooke incident - what a hunting! I noticed it at once, it was really too evident. The man & his music is really entirely unsympathetic to me & I also distrust him entirely. Did you receive 3 copies of my "Mass" which I had sent to you from Berlin? Of course I shall be in London for the performance of "Paris" & then we can hear Brigg fair in the 3½ & go to Hanley for the 2nd. Don't forget that we expect you to return here with me. I have ordered my tickets already for the Bal des Quat'z Arts from an artist friend of mine. My wife hopes that Mrs Bantock will also be able to come. I want to make a slight alteration

A letter from Delius to the English composer and conductor Granville Bantock, 1908

in the score of "Brigg fair" : 8 Bars before the
$\frac{3}{2}$ at the end . I have it only in my head, but
I believe a better crescendo could be obtained
by ~~omitting~~ the Harmonies half a bar not
~~in that is~~ in every bar

Something like the above . It could be altered
in the rehearsal easy enough. Who has the
Score now ? I received several very good paper
notices about "Brigg fair". Do you know that I have
never in my life heard "L'après Midi d'un Faune
or seen the music. Farewell, dear friend
& let me hear all about the Musical League.
By the Bye "Baughan in his criticism in ~~Holbrooks~~
piece "Apollo the Seaman" wrote, " Mr Holbrookes clever
& picturesque score " & " we have no doubt that
Mr Holbrookes music ~~rend doub~~ renders the expression
of the poem as a whole " or something to that effect.
That is criticism with a vengeance !! I should not
like to have written that as a musical critic —

~~kindest remembrance to your wife~~

Affectionately yours
Frederick Delius

written to Ethel Smyth), Debussy and Ravel were the only composers who shared in some measure the refinement and taste of his own ideals. He had studied Debussy for orchestration, Ravel for the balance of choir and orchestra and certainly his string quartet. For the rest I believe he went his own way—but he needed solitude to pursue it. The remoteness of French rural life may be gauged by the English miniaturist I met in Marlotte who had lived there as long as Delius at Grez and never even heard of him!

His two most persuasive supporters in England now made their appearance separately at Grez to persuade him to agree to a festival of his music which one of them, Sir Thomas Beecham, planned to celebrate in the autumn of 1929. The other, Philip Heseltine, was given the preliminary task of sounding Delius on the project. Heseltine had been an invaluable help in making piano scores of choral works, an opera, and four-hand arrangements for piano duet of many of Delius's orchestral works before they had been recorded, besides writing his admirable study of Delius. Sir Thomas Beecham, the foremost champion and acknowledged exponent of Delius's art, then arrived to outline the programmes and invite Delius and Jelka to be his guests at the festival. Delius hesitated, but was persuaded to accept.

Later Sir Thomas wrote to Delius asking if he had an unpublished work for voice and orchestra to include as a novelty in the programmes. Piles of faded pencil sketches (all in full score) had accumulated from a lifetime's work. Along with the sketches of *Songs of Sunset* was one I could not place. On playing it over to Delius he recognized it immediately as a setting for baritone and orchestra of Dowson's best-known poem *Cynara* which he had abandoned, indeed quite forgotten, after judging its inclusion inappropriate in the scheme of *Songs of Sunset* for which it was intended initially. It was complete in every detail up to the words 'Then falls thy shadow, Cynara', at which there was a blank. Delius decided to fill it, and, after some painful and frustrating hours of work, managed to complete the remaining bars. I shall never forget my thrill when I took down the telling chord on the trombones on the final word 'Cynara'!

The success of this dictation was as crucial to Delius as to me. If it failed to sound well in performance he would give up trying to compose altogether. *A Late Lark*, with words by Henley, for tenor and orchestra was completed similarly and performed at the festival.

X

Final Phase and Death

From now on until the day of his death Delius never left Grez-sur-Loing. The success of the festival brought great satisfaction. There had been public acclaim and evidence of respect on all sides for his artistic integrity and achievement from critics and professional musicians. What now remained was to finish his life's work with my help. Hearing the completed *A Late Lark* and *Cynara* in rehearsal had given him renewed confidence in himself and, what was equally important, in me. The sound of chorus and orchestra in the concert-room had thrilled him to the core; he had even dared to hope that somehow some day he might complete that other and final choral work that irked his mind, but which was then no more advanced than the opening bars of each movement. There was much to be done before that could be attempted. Delius had set his heart on writing a third sonata for violin and piano. Here, too, were pencilled scraps jotted down and almost forgotten. He was so ill when he began to dictate the sonata that I almost despaired of the day-to-day threading of effort and thought essential to the making of a coherent whole.

The weather, too, was depressing. Heavy rains had flooded the river till the whole landscape was awash and it was scarcely light. By the second week in February the music was flowing and *flow* was the operative word with Delius. I was fearful at first of these sessions in the music-room for each time it meant facing the unknown, and that was not easy with a man like Delius. To the end I never lost my awe of him; there was a presence about him always.

'I'll work today'—that was a signal I awaited each lunch-time, for the room had to be prepared for his coming, the temperature just right, and his arm-chair positioned beside the piano. When he was ready, and not until, each pair of double doors was opened along the corridors by the servants and his wife sent ahead for the final inspection. If she approved, the procession began. The male nurse would heave him over his shoulder from which he hung limp and helpless, and stagger up the steep, polished stairs from the living-room and through his bedroom and passage-ways into the music-room—slumping him into the chair. Then when the two of them had got their breath, adjustments to cushions and feet were made and we were left alone to work.

We began by my playing what already existed; then came the moment I dreaded most—the pause as I waited for what he might do! By now he had changed from the paralyzed figure propped up beside me to an upright, excitable, gesticulating fighter as he felt himself deeper and deeper into the music with more and more frenzied intensity, calling out the notes, their values in time, the pitch, the phrase-lengths whilst I struggled at the keyboard to reproduce them and jot them down in manuscript. He always dictated with great rapidity and was peeved if his meaning was not grasped immediately. Verbal or musical repetition incensed him equally at this stage of his life.

By comparison with what was to follow, the sonata was not difficult to take down in this way; by Easter of 1930 it was finished. Delius then sent for May Harrison, the violinist, to come and play the work to him. She with her talented sister Beatrice, the cellist, had previously given the first performance of his Concerto for Violin, Cello and Orchestra; it was composed and expressly dedicated to them. May Harrison arrived and we played him his new sonata: not one note had to be altered.

This is the best of the three sonatas to introduce young players to Delius. A few observations about his music, applicable to the opening of the sonata, may not be out of place here. The secret of Delius is *controlled rubato*; pointing the phrases on operative beats—robbing Peter to pay Paul—within the time-rate of a bar without pulling the music about unnecessarily. First one must feel oneself totally involved and moving to the fluid pulse. The printed page in Delius's case is an elusive guide to its realization; his phrase-lengths are free and often irregular and the musical sense is apt to elude one if not felt intuitively. Rarely in his music is the first beat of a bar the important pulse. Up-beats, particularly the last of a bar, are the ones to nurse rather than down-beats. In his long-drawn phrases of melodic prose one should always 'go' for the operative note and this is not generally the highest note, for Delius had a strange habit of overleaping his climaxes before reaching them.

Now let us look at the first paragraph of the Sonata No. 3. Bearing in mind the long fourth up-beat, the *third* is the operative beat for the pianist (even though the sounds have already been made in bars 1–3 on

Above left, Delius and his wife at the Langham Hotel, London, 1929; *above right*, bust of Delius by his wife

Below, the dining-room at Grez

Percy and Ella Grainger with Balfour Gardener in Delius's garden at Grez

Below, the composer's wife, Jelka

depressing the keys on the previous beat) and continues so as far as bar 7 when the stress falls here on the *last* beat of the bar. Begin a shade slower than the marked tempo of = 76. Delius loves to steal in on the ear not assault it. Asterisks mark the operative beats the violinist should go for and lean on with feeling until reaching the *first-beat* accentuation at the climactic new figure announced at bar 12:

From Sonata No. 3 for Violin and Piano

If the melodic line is pointed in this way the pianist should sense by the 'pull' of the chords the weight and manner of his contribution.

A Song of Summer had already revealed the problems and difficulties of dictating orchestral music. Delius, as I have said, rarely made a piano sketch to orchestrate afterwards. It had been his habit from the first to complete every detail of orchestration straightway into the orchestral score though it was done after 'placing' the sounds at the keyboard. I doubt if he heard his piano as such but coloured it imaginatively in orchestral tones. He wrote very little for the piano itself.

Songs of Farewell was an alarming prospect. I shall never forget that crucial day nor the old autocrat's instructions to take 32 stave manuscript-paper and set out the score for 1st & 2nd flutes with piccolo; 1st & 2nd oboes and cor anglais; 1st & 2nd clarinets and bass clarinet; 1st & 2nd bassoons and double bassoon; 1st & 2nd and 3rd & 4th French horns; 1st, 2nd & 3rd trumpets; 1st, 2nd & 3rd trombones and bass tuba; percussion and harp; sopranos, altos, tenors and basses divided into eight parts; 1st & 2nd violins, violas, cellos and double-basses adding 'and I'll tell you in advance when the strings are to be sub-divided!'

He then asked me to read aloud the words of the poems which Jelka had

88

selected and copied out from Walt Whitman's *Leaves of Grass*; she had been keeping them for years hopefully waiting for this moment. There was a pause; his relaxed manner left him and he began to dictate.

There were further complications now; the complexity of thinking in so many strands often all at once; the problems of orchestral and vocal balance; the wider areas of possible misunderstandings in the transposing instruments which sound different notes from those written. Delius was carried away exhausted after each of these gruelling sessions of work and was physically incapable of more effort by the time the choral work was finished.

I left him therefore to rest contented whilst I went to London to arrange with Ralph Hawkes for the publication of the new scores he had written in this way. I was somewhat unnerved to find that Delius had agreed to Hawkes's firm intention to print and put these works on sale before Delius himself had heard them in performance even by high-powered radio.

Two other short works were yet to come, *Caprice & Elegy* for cello and chamber orchestra which he composed for Beatrice Harrison as a novelty for her American tour and a short orchestral piece *Fantastic Dance* which he dedicated, perhaps appropriately, to me!

There yet remained one other task, to play him all his unpublished works; he would decide which, if any, were worth revising. A prelude from the opera *Irmelin* (1890–92) was improved with adjustments to the middle section. The best music from another opera *Margot-la-Rouge* (1902) was salvaged and with the aid of Robert Nichols—poet, friend and lover of his music— Delius transformed it into the *Idyll* for soprano, baritone and orchestra to a selection of words again from Walt Whitman.

Delius continued to receive a few visitors, notably Elgar who had flown to Paris to conduct his concerto played by Menuhin. Two men so different it would be difficult to name, particularly in their prime. This can be heard in their music. Much of Elgar's has the quality of a smooth-running engine, an elegant car, hugging the highways of the English countryside, the regulated streets of cathedral cities and always seen on state occasions. Delius's conveyance is like no other, self-propelled and largely home-made; it is seen in cities only at night or in the most unusual places—the swamps of Florida, the mountains of Norway but rarely in England, being serviced and garaged in rural France. Of their meeting it may be said that they got on better in their seventies than would have been credible in their forties. Their opinions of each other's music when Elgar had *The Apostles* and *The Music Makers* and Delius *Sea-Drift* included in the programme of the Birmingham Musical

89

Festival of 1912 had been forgotten. 'I found Elgar's music dull and interminable, colourless and thickly orchestrated. His attitude to mine was slightly censorial as if he considered it not quite proper!' The two continued to correspond in the friendliest terms until Elgar's death in the spring of 1934.

Each of the new works had now been published and heard in public in London; *A Song of Summer* by Sir Henry Wood at a Promenade Concert in September 1931; *Songs of Farewell* by Dr. Malcolm Sargent (as he was then) at a Courtauld-Sargent Concert in March 1932; the *Idyll* by Sir Henry Wood (with Dora Labette and Roy Henderson as soloists) at a Promenade Concert in October 1933; and *Fantastic Dance* by Dr. (now Sir) Adrian Boult at a BBC Symphony Concert in January 1934.

My work for Delius now seemed ended and I left Grez with the promise that I would return whenever he needed me. Despite his feebleness and hopeless condition with Jelka's care and equable nature there was reason to suppose he would go on living like this for many years. Nor had the daily strain on Jelka worried me unduly; she was very strong and had good help and the Brooks family were always at hand. She had a voluminous correspondence which she so obviously enjoyed except writing her 'thunder letters to publishers'!

I was quite unprepared for the telegram that hastened my recall. She was to be operated on the following day at Fontainebleau!

I arrived to find her out of danger but Delius distressed and looking frailer. He seemed more cheerful, however, when I moved into his room but was little disposed to talk. All he wanted was the incessant murmur of my voice reading aloud. His *In a Summer Garden* roused him encouragingly but he asked me to continue with *Huckleberry Finn* the moment it was over! Within a fortnight he had a decided relapse and begged me to wire for Balfour Gardiner. By now in addition to his nurse's efforts with German translations of Edgar Wallace, I had intoned almost all the works of Mark Twain through nine hours a day and half the night! Gardiner came in great agitation only to find Delius quite normal again; there was champagne for lunch in the room downstairs and Delius instructed Gardiner about his practical affairs, particularly in the event of his or Jelka's death. Gardiner had gone but an hour on his way back to London when I noticed a sudden decline in Delius. Within a few hours he was sinking fast and the doctor was on call constantly. In a last effort to revive him Jelka was brought back home from hospital but he died in the early hours of Sunday, 10th June 1934.

A temporary burial was arranged in the village cemetery because of

Jelka's illness. He had hoped all along to be buried in his garden but a change in French law had recently forbidden it. He had been persuaded finally that Limpsfield in Surrey would be a suitable resting-place, a decision I have always regretted since.

Delius, free from national prejudices, had played no part in English life beyond visits to London to hear his music. Unless urged by Beecham or Heseltine he had remained outside English musical politics making no effort to promote his works and having no faith in organizations. He had accustomed himself to a rural existence in which he was happiest in solitude with friends to stay from time to time. 'I would have hated an English village with institutes of this and that and the vicar for ever on the doorstep. No one would dream of disturbing me in France. I have worked without interruption as I pleased and not been regarded as an oddity.'

The countryside round Grez had nurtured his genius and given him peace to pursue his ideals and realize on paper his meditations in Norway. This, despite his aloofness from the French, was the place in which he was happiest of all and this, I think, is where he belonged.

Epilogue

I spent the following Christmas with Jelka at Grez and later in the year returned to complete the arrangements for the exhumation of Delius's coffin and accompany it by motor-hearse to Bologne and then by boat to Folkestone. It was almost midnight when we reached Limpsfield where his body was interred by lantern-light. The next day, Sunday, Sir Thomas Beecham conducted a small chamber orchestra in some of the master's miniatures in the church and afterwards delivered an oration to the vast assembly gathered round the grave. Jelka, now a mortally sick woman, had made the journey to England separately with her cook, but was unable to attend the funeral. Within a few days she too was laid to rest at Limpsfield.

Differences had arisen after Delius's death involving Jelka, Sir Thomas Beecham and Balfour Gardiner. Delius had wished his then meagre royalties to be used to give an annual concert of works by unknown British composers with one work of his own. Beecham had argued that this was impracticable; that the Patron's Fund of the Royal College of Music already existed for this purpose. He persuaded Jelka that a Trust should be set up instead to further the cause of Delius's music. He then brought in his own solicitor to help Jelka establish the Trust. The Trust consists of a legal trustee, a bank trustee and three musical advisers. Since its inception it has sponsored gramophone recordings of almost every printed work by Delius, the publication of new editions of certain scores, and given assistance to concert societies needing extra orchestral rehearsals in the preparation of the music for public performances. Gardiner, though supporting the project in principle, was deeply hurt nevertheless that Delius's wish should have been disregarded and withdrew in disgust. For years he had been Delius's closest friend. He had purchased the house from Delius when the composer was in financial difficulties, subject to the Deliuses having the right to continue living there until the death of the survivor. On Jelka's death he had sold the

Above left, Jelka Delius; *above right*, the composer's wife (centre) with Ella
and Percy Grainger in 1929

Below, Delius and his wife in 1933

Above, Solano Grove, Florida as it is today; *below*, Eric Fenby with the composer in 1932

place, but I doubt if he would ever have done so had the Deliuses been buried in the cemetery at Grez.

Thirty-three years were to pass before I set foot in Grez again. Inevitably all is changed. The house has been charmingly renovated and the garden formalized by the present owners, Professor and Madame Merle d'Aubigné. No trace of the music-room remains. Delius's meadow across the Loing is edged with tiny weekend chalets and the noble stone bridge that spans the river now carries the indignity of a wooden super-structure, a relic of the last war. All that is left of his and Jelka's upwards of forty years residence here is the paint-smeared door of her studio and the picture postcards in the village store with the inscription '*Maison de Frederick DESLIUS—compositeur anglais, décédé dans cette maison le 10 juin 1934.*' The French who ignored his music in his lifetime have even misspelt his name in death!

The greatest change of all is the sound of children at play in the walled garden of his home where he loved to sit in silence.

Suggestions for Further Reading

Delius: a critical biography by Arthur Hutchings (Macmillan)

Delius as I Knew Him by Eric Fenby (Icon Books)

Delius: in *A Composers Eleven* by Neville Cardus (Cape)

Frederick Delius by Philip Heseltine and Hubert Foss (Bodley Head)

Frederick Delius by Thomas Beecham (Hutchinson)

Frederick Delius: a discography by Stuart Upton and Malcolm Walker (Delius Society)

Frederick Delius: Memories of my Brother by Clare Black (Nicholson & Watson), now out of print but available from libraries

The Songs of Delius by A. K. Holland (O.U.P.)

Summary of Principal Works of Delius

Choral Works

Appalachia	1902
Sea-Drift	1903
A Mass of Life	1904–5
Songs of Sunset	1906–7
An Arabesque	1911
A Song of the High Hills	1911–12
Requiem	1914–16
Songs of Farewell	1931

Orchestral Works

Paris: The Song of a Great City	1899
Brigg Fair	1907
In a Summer Garden	1908
Life's Dance (second revision of *The Dance Goes On*)	1911
Summer Night on the River	1911
On Hearing the First Cuckoo in Spring	1912
North Country Sketches	1913–14
Dance Rhapsody No. 2	1916
Eventyr	1917
A Song before Sunrise	1918
A Song of Summer	1928–30

Solo Instruments and Orchestra

Concerto for Piano and Orchestra	1906
Concerto for Violin, Cello and Orchestra	1915–16

Summary of Principal Works of Delius

Concerto for Violin and Orchestra   1916
Concerto for Cello and Orchestra   1921

Chamber Music

Sonata for Violin and Piano No. 1   1905–14
String Quartet   1916–17
Sonata for Cello and Piano   1917
Sonata for Violin and Piano No. 2   1924
Sonata for Violin and Piano No. 3   1930

Operas

Irmelin   MS   1890–92
The Magic Fountain   MS   1893
Koanga   1895–97
A Village Romeo and Juliet   1900–01
Margot-la-Rouge   1902
Fennimore and Gerda   1908–10

Incidental Music

Folkeraadet   MS   1897
Hassan   1920

Unaccompanied part-songs and over sixty solo songs.

Index

97

Index

Index

Index